Smoked Mixology

The Essential Cocktail Recipes Book
for Classical and Smoked Cocktails,
Innovative Home Bartending Techniques,
Tools, Ingredients & Practical Tips
to Master Captivating Drinks

Headley Sullivan

Chapter One: Introduction

Who is this book for?

This book is for those who are curious not only about mixology and the art of making cocktails, but about how to create a new kind of cocktail. Smoked cocktails have stolen the hearts and fascinated the minds of bartenders and mixologists everywhere. If you also want to jump on this craze, this book will give you the know-how, plus the tips and tricks you need to be a successful mixologist of smoked cocktails. And if you have no idea what a smoked cocktail is, this book is for you too. I will walk you through everything you need to know about making cocktails, share how to best prepare a recipe with the correct measurements and all the tools you need to create your cocktails successfully. You'll be able to hit the ground running.

Ultimately, this book is written for cocktail enthusiasts, and those interested in home bartending. If you are someone who has been playing around with how to make different kinds of drinks to share with your friends, and anyone who wants to experiment and learn something new, this book is for you. There is also going to be a section written all about non-alcoholic smoked drinks for those who want the experience but don't imbibe.

Table of Contents

Chapter One: Introduction

    Who is this book for?

    What is a cocktail?

    The world of smoking cocktails

    How to use units of measurement

    The smoked mixology toolkit

Chapter Two: It's cocktails time

    A brief history of the success of cocktails

    Evolution of cocktails

    Curiosities about cocktails

Chapter Three: The beauty of Mixology

    What is Mixology?

    The secret of a perfect cocktail

    Home and flair bartending

    Cocktails and most important spirits you should know for smoked cocktails

Chapter Four: Smoked cocktails: the new frontier

    Smoking technique and equipment

    Wood, syrups, fruits and seeds to choose

Chapter Five: Smoked cocktails recipes

Chapter Six: Notes

Chapter Seven: Conclusion

What is a cocktail?

Invented in 1860, the cocktail came about at the birth of what has become the modern bar and the publishing of *How to Mix Drinks: A Bon Vivant's Companion*. This book gave cocktail enthusiasts the ability to start making mixed drinks at home. Preparing cocktails would become a staple of home entertainment for the next 100 years. But we'll talk more about that later.

A *cocktail* is a mixed drink often made with a distilled liquor. You might be familiar with distilled liquors like gin, brandy, and vodka, but you can also make a cocktail with ingredients like arrack, cachaça, rum, tequila, or whiskey. Whatever you choose, liquor is the base ingredient and it is mixed with other delicious ingredients or garnishments of your choice. It all depends on the cocktail recipe. And many recipes have been perfected over the centuries.

The world of smoking cocktails

Many patrons of bars, bartenders and mixologists agreed that cocktails needed a new trend to get people excited about them again. These mixologists were a little bored too. They thought they had exhausted their experimentation with adding flowers, herbs, and bitters. They wanted something new to try and a different taste. Many realized that there is already a smoky taste to some spirits, such as mezcal. In fact, with the taste already in their mouths, lovers of the classic, bourbon-based Old-Fashioned often request theirs made with mezcal. So mixologists and bartenders alike want to deliver on the tastes that patrons are asking for.

Mixologists didn't expect how this innovative kind of cocktail would expand their own vocabularies and tastes. The smoky flavor is not overwhelming, and is simply, surprisingly pleasant, bringing the taste of the outdoors, indoors. That campfire-feel, year- round, in your favorite drink provides a warm, fuzzy feeling that would amp up anyone's buzz. Familiar ingredients are mixed in less familiar ways, which excites bartenders and mixologists. They can do more with a cocktail without reinventing the wheel.

Smoked cocktails started in New York City and they caught on, gaining popularity all over. Now wherever you go, there are smoked cocktails on the menu. The world of smoked cocktails is now wide open and quite prevalent. And what an exciting world it is, even for a beginner!

In this book, you will learn how to make your own smoked cocktail and be the envy of your friends. Even though you usually find smoked cocktails on the menus of swanky bars staffed with brilliantly skilled mixologists, with the right tools, ingredients, and recipes, you too can bring the world of smoked cocktails to your home! To help you, we've provided some commonly used ingredients and useful information below:

THE EDIBLE GARNISHMENTS TYPICALLY USED

Fruits	Spices	Vegetables	Miscellaneous
Star anise	Sugar, granulated or powdered	Cocktail olives (often stuffed with pimentos)	Shrimp
Strawberries	Candied ginger	Carrot sticks	Bitters dashed onto egg-white foam
Watermelon wedges	Cinnamon, grated	Celery stalks (usually with leaves attached)	Edible flowers
Lemon slices, twists, or wedges	Mint sprigs or leaves	Cocktail onions	
Lime slices, twists, or wedges	Nutmeg, grated		
Maraschino cherries	Pepper		
Orange slices, twists, or wedges	Salt, coarse (applied to the rim of glasses)		

**EXTRA DECORATION OR DRAMATIC FLAIR - INEDIBLE GARNISHMENTS
TYPICALLY USED**

Decorative	Dramatic
Flags	Sparklers
Plastic animals (attached to the rim of the glass)	Inedible flowers
Plastic swords	Candles
Bead necklaces (especially common during Mardi Gras and Carnival)	Fire (see Flaming beverage)
Drinking straws (colorful or unusually shaped)	Smoke (hence the smoked cocktail)
Cocktail umbrellas	

Flavorings such as one or more types of juice, fruit, honey, milk or cream, or spices can also be added. Or, use one or more of these simple syrups to create various flavorings:

Single flavor	Combination flavor
Rose Simple Syrup	Rosemary–Clove Simple Syrup
Fresh Mint Simple Syrup	Blackberry-Lavender Syrup
Thai Chile Simple Syrup	Lavender-Thyme Syrup
Maylay-Spiced Syrup	
Black Pepper Syrup	

How to use units of measurement

Refer to the following chart when trying to determine exactly how to measure your cocktails. These are units of volume or capacity showing the quantity your containers can hold. Please note: *ml* is the abbreviation for a *milliliter*; *L* represents a *liter.* These are the metric units of liquid. The US standard or customary units are ounce (oz., or fluid ounces, fl. oz.), cup (c.), pint (pt.) quart (qt.), and gallon (gal).

When using the chart keep the following formulas in mind:

1000 ml	1 L
1 cup	8 fluid ounces
1 pint	2 cups
1 quart	2 cups
1 quart	2 pints
1 gallon	4 quarts

2 tablespoons	1 fl. oz.	30 mL
1/4 cup	2 fl. oz.	60 mL
1/2 cup	4 fl. oz.	120 mL
1 cup	8 fl. oz.	240 mL
1 1/2 cups	12 fl. oz.	355 mL
2 cups or 1 pint	16 fl. oz.	475 mL
4 cups or 1 quart	32 fl. oz.	1 L
1 gallon	128 fl. oz.	4 L

(tablespoons = tbsp)

When making cocktails, it is important to have special tools of preparation. These include:

Rolling Pin	Drink Disk
Bar Knife	Shaker (Boston, Cobbler, Parisian)
Chopping Board	Jigger (Large, Small, Stepped)
Citrus Peeler	Stirrer/Bar Spoon/Mixing Glass

The smoked mixology toolkit

Comprehensive and effective smoking kits have preferably been put together and distributed by bartenders and mixologists who know what they are doing. They find and put together the best products out there and know which ones will last and work most efficiently. With a quick on line search, you will find many companies who make and distribute smoking kits. If you want some advice on what to look out for, keep some of the following things in mind:

First, you want to find a kit that has many reviews and at least a four-star rating. This will ensure the products have been purchased and used by other cocktail enthusiasts who can tell you whether or not the products work. Look for reviews for items purchased by fellow novice home bartenders. Their reviews will tell you what kits are best to learn on, and which ones have the most ease of use and not a steep learning curve. You don't want to purchase products that are difficult to use. You also want to look for reviews from people who are more skilled in the world of mixology. These reviews will tell you if you can use the kit to create the kind of cocktails that will please the taster. If you read a bad review from a mixologist who says the product doesn't perform properly, or the kit is missing key items, do not purchase that kit.

Second, do your best to buy a kit with the most items included. If you can purchase most of your items in one place, that'll ultimately save you time and money, and you won't have to wait and find all the items you need before you get started. Just as making a regular cocktail requires special tools, so does the smoked cocktail. Look for a kit that has every product a mixologist deems necessary, which will give you the most bang for your buck.

You can find descriptions of these items and the purpose they serve in the following sections.

Portable Carrying Case/Smoking kit

The American-made Cocktail Smoking Kit from Middleton Mixology features a SmokeTop cap, a torch lighter, and premium food-grade smoking chips in four different flavors. This is a good example of a kit that will contain everything you need to take a beginner's crack at smoking a cocktail. But if you need a more comprehensive kit, look for ones that have these items or more. You may opt to simply buy a smoke infuser or cocktail smoker. These will most often come with wood chips to light. They usually aren't scented or fancy, but they get the job done.

You might be wondering why a smoking kit would have a portable carrying case. First, you might want to use the case to keep everything stored properly. These durable cases will ensure your items have a longer shelf life and can prevent any accidental damage or wear and tear. The second—and fun—reason is that a portable carrying case allows you to take your kit to parties or events where you plan on showing off your expertise. You might even want to take your case on vacation with you!

Smoke boards (Such as the White Oak Smoke Board)

Typically available in cedar, oak, cherry and hickory, smoke boards or flavored-plank boards are an important item in your toolkit. Using them is an easy and reliable way to add wonderful flavors and the aromas of smoked wood to every single, perfectly-crafted cocktail. It's recommended you collect a few varieties of smoke boards, because often, different recipes may call for different wood-smoke flavors. Using the boards is an easy two-step process. First, you can burn the board with a butane torch. Second, you cover with a glass–preferably a rocks glass, so it's best to have a few of these on hand–to trap in the smoke and bathe the glass. Again, this is just one way to use them with the rest of your kit.

Smoking box

If you want to get really serious about cocktail smoking, purchasing a smoking box is the high-end approach. A smoking box is for the serious student of mixology who wants an opportunity to show what they are made of. Expect to pay more for one of these than you might for an entire cocktail smoking kit, which is often less than half the price. Consider finding one that is compatible with other products you can use, such as an infuser that can hook up to the smoking box. This, as I will discuss, might be the safest way to create smoke. You want to look for a box that has many positive consumer reviews, but read the reviews carefully. Often, you might find that someone using it didn't exactly know how to use it, or didn't smoke the correct cocktail with it. You want to find an easy-to-use box that doesn't have a steep learning curve. Using a smoking box takes practice, and often works best with certain types of recipes. But once you get skilled in using one, you might never look back.

Smoking gun

A decent smoking kit might have one of these included, but if you plan on purchasing it separately, you might be surprised at how inexpensive they are compared to other items. Again, use caution when looking for the perfect smoking gun. What you want to look for is one that is safe to use, and one that doesn't break down or stop working after a few uses. Many recipes are best made with a smoking gun and they can be safe and easy if you properly read the instructions and take care when using one.

Smoking dome

Smoking domes can range in price, so it might be best to do some research and see what you are paying for. Many people have found that the dome effect can be created in other ways and may not require a high-end smoking dome to create the same effect. So take a close look at the reviews, and see which ones don't seem too complicated to use. Many times, domes will come with extra items, so keep a lookout for those as well. Some mixologists suggest that a smoking dome and a smoking box are essentially the same thing, so keep that in mind when you do any kind of price shopping or when you are deciding what to include in your home bar station. Others simply have combined a sturdy wooden block and a glass cake dome, the kind usually used to keep bakery items fresh. So it might be useful to get creative, but also play it safe since a cake dome isn't made to be used with heat! Ultimately, I suggest purchasing items that are proven to be safe to use.

Handheld Kitchen Torch

The handheld kitchen torch is a useful item to have on hand for easy lighting. Easier and safer than striking a match, a kitchen torch can be used to add a flame to your chips, sticks and boards. If the butane is not included but the butane refill works you can find it at all local hardware stores.

Large-mouthed Mason Jar

If you don't want to opt for using an expensive smoking dome, you can obtain large-mouthed mason jars, which are really great for trapping in smoky flavor. Mason jars can also be used to easily stir cocktails or for serving drinks in a decorative way reminiscent of summer, beaches and pool parties, and are a delightful tool for drinking outdoors on a sunny day.

Some important tools to have on hand when creating the cocktails you wish to smoke:

Straight Plating Tongs

Plating tongs look like large tweezers. They come in various sizes for various uses. It is most professional to use these when placing a garnish instead of your bare fingers.

Tweezers

Use tweezers for the most precise of placements. It can also help you to move and place different or delicate garnishes without fumbling or crushing them.

Grater

Often used to grate cheese, a grater can also be used to mince herbs and fruits for when the recipe calls for it.

Citrus Planer/Zester

A planer or zester allows you to remove the zest from citrus. Planers help in removing the zest from citrus fruits while leaving behind the fruit's bitter white pith. You will find these definitely come in handy as many cocktails call for citrus fruits.

Paring Knife

Unlike your typical kitchen knife, you can use a precise paring knife to peel or cut fruit and vegetables into very small pieces, or to carry out other similar precision work that might be necessary for adding ingredients or creating garnishes.

Swiss Peeler

This kind of peeler will remove the skin from fruits and vegetables more easily than a knife. The most high-end kind comes with a carbon steel blade that doesn't need sharpening. I recommend obtaining one with an ergonomic design that works in the right or left hand.

8-inch Pinking Shears

Often used for precise fabric design cutting, pinking shears are used by skilled bartenders and mixologists to create interesting designs in their garnishes. You can learn different ways to experiment with cutting and use these versatile shears to do the work.

What to Look for in a Garnishing Tool

Primarily, there are three easy things: fit, sturdiness, and sharpness. This goes for all of the above tools listed. If they feel nice in your hand and you can be dexterous with them, then you will be more likely to use them and more likely to perfect your skills.

Tool kits

Tool kits are an inexpensive way to obtain all of the tools you need in one shot. Also look for the best reviewed kits.

3-in-1 tools

The same goes for any item that contains more than one tool. This makes it easier to store your items and makes them more easily portable if you want to take them with you.

Different kinds of chips to smoke:

The smoke you use enhances the scent and flavor of every cocktail and gives the drinker the sense that they are next to an open fire or camping outdoors. It's a feeling many smoked cocktail enthusiasts have come to crave. Quality smoking chips (once again, check reviews), often come in separate kits, packaged and prepped and ready to use. Often you will choose which type to purchase based on what your recipe calls for, but you can also use the kits to experiment with flavors that evoke certain experiences or environments. I recommend you have a variety of kits to create different kinds of experiences. Often, these experiences, paired with particular recipes, are seasonal. People often tie emotions to these sense memories from different seasons and it further enhances their enjoyment of the cocktail.

Apple Chips

Smoking cocktails is all about the experience, and what better way than to evoke apple orchards and falling leaves of autumn? Apple chips are often paired with hickory, maple, and cinnamon to give the flavor, warmth and feel of fall outdoors.

Pecan Chips

Often paired with maple and sweeter fruits, like peaches, this gives a dessert-feel to the drink. It's reminiscent of taking a hot pie out of the oven during the winter holidays. (Is your mouth watering yet?)

Cherry Chips

Used often when smoking a bourbon or brandy, the cherry flavor can give the feel of a cold winter's night, but if the fruit taste is enhanced with other cherry flavors it can also have a summery feel. This versatile chip is definitely worth having on hand.

Hickory Chips, Maple Chips, Oak Chips

Great for pairing with other flavored chips, these give the "woody" feel you are looking for when burning to create smoke. Oak is for those denser, woodier tastes, while maple and hickory are great while serving up cocktail recipes that pair wonderfully with mesquite barbeque on a hot summer day.

There are many other types of chips available. These are just a few suggestions and favorites but look for others to create your own smoked cocktail experiences.

Best practices when using these items:

Cleaning

Clean with a damp cloth and air dry. Often these items are not dishwasher safe and any wood might have a tendency to warp if not cleaned properly. Fancier products are often finished with oils, as to ensure they last a good while and though they are durable, treat them with care to ensure their longevity.

Safety

For safety sake, it's always best to thoroughly read any directions on the items you purchase. And on that note, if they do not come with instructions, I suggest searching for items that do. Also, keep in mind that professional mixologists or skilled home bartenders you may know didn't know how to use these items overnight. In fact, many mixologists say that using items such as a smoking gun or dome takes ample practice. So start out slowly.

It's suggested that you learn in an area of your home, or even outside, where there is a less chance of the room filling up with smoke or something going awry. While there is little chance of this happening, it's best to give this a few rounds of practice before "performing" in front of others. Ensure your items do not get too hot. Practice fire safety by ensuring that only the item you are lighting becomes lit. A good safety precaution to have is to have heat-resistant gloves and water on standby, as well as a fire extinguisher nearby. You're creating small fires, but accidents happen; it's best to ensure safety for yourself and others by being prepared for a larger event, just in case.

Replacements

It's also best to ensure that you can get replacements for any items you purchase. It's unfortunate, but sometimes you get a defective smoking gun that doesn't produce smoke, or a cocktail smoking block that doesn't seem to be creating any smoke. When this happens, check the reviews. See if the items are outright defective, or if there might be an issue with the product. When cleaning certain items, it is important to be sure you are performing the maintenance properly by unclogging them or scraping off any residue that might collect. Know that some smoking guns often come with replacement parts. You can contact the seller, or return to the ad to see if any of these items were included in your original kit. This is one reason why it is best to purchase a fully-stocked kit that would include many of the items you need.

Beginner bartenders

Throughout the book, I will be giving you tips on how to be a master bartender and a skilled mixologist. There are tips and tricks for every beginner to learn. Bartending can be intimidating if you are new to it; with practice, you will become skilled in no time. First, remember that there is more to bartending than serving drinks. Knowing where all of the items you need and what they do is a great first step. Become familiar with your tools. Later on in the book, I will be sharing with you more and more tools you will need to learn how to use, so by the end you will be an expert and have a tool kit of your own. Remember, no one is perfect at anything the first time they do it. You are bound to make mistakes. The thing to keep in mind is that each mistake, especially when mixing cocktail recipes, is an opportunity to learn what not to do. If you forget an ingredient, mix the wrong things together, break or spill--it's okay! Every seasoned bartender made all of these mistakes when they first started out.

It helps if you keep things clean and organized! If you keep things clean they won't get sticky, you won't have any big infestations (yuck) and the space will be more appealing to your guests. If you have everything at the ready, it's easy to remember what you need to use.

Learn how to pour. People notice a good pour, and when you do it right, it makes you look all the more skilled at what you are doing. Also, you won't waste anything if you pour just the right amount, and liquor is expensive!

Memorize some recipes. This way you aren't always referring back to charts, or trying to remember something you forgot. You will feel more confident too when you can call up a recipe on the spot in front of someone, even if it's your family member or friend.

Learn to talk while you are doing things. Again, it makes the experience less-nerve wracking for everyone, including yourself. You've probably heard the term fake it till you make it; act confident and you will feel more relaxed and confident. Being able to hold a conversation through your mix and pour will definitely give you the look and the feel of a seasoned pro! To get you started, the next chapter gives you some facts and history about cocktails to get you started with a topic to share while you show off your new skills.

Chapter Two: It's Cocktail Time

A brief history of the success of cocktails

The debate rages on about the origins of the word *cocktail*. But the first recorded mention of a cocktail as a beverage appeared in the American book, *The Farmers Cabinet*, in 1803. The cocktail was first defined specifically as an alcoholic beverage three years later in *The Balance and Columbian Repository* on May 13, 1806. Cocktail ingredients traditionally included spirits, sugar, water and bitters. However, this definition evolved throughout the 1800s, and in modern times includes the addition of a liqueur.

The technical evolution of cocktails goes through stages, mostly of experimentation, out of necessity for new medicines, or simply their glamor and appeal. From fermenting jars of honey and added spice to make delicious concoctions, to the cock & bull tales and Cock Ales of 16th Century Britain, the evolution of cocktails has a unique and storied past. But cocktails did not only exist in one corner of the world.

South Americans stored mixed liquids in primitive vessels, which taught them all about the methods of fermentation and creating a mixed alcoholic drink. During excavation and archeological digs in the banks of Tigris, five-thousand-year-old Mesopotamian earthenware was discovered containing traces of tartaric acid, honey, apple juice and barley which has been recorded as the first known and earliest example of a mixed alcoholic drink in human history.

But many say the cocktail as we know it today didn't truly exist until Jerry Thomas published a bartenders' guide called *How to Mix Drinks: The Bon Vivant's Companion* in 1862. The book included ten cocktail recipes using bitters, which differentiated them from other alcoholic beverages like punches and cobblers. Today, we know that the addition of bitters is what designates a true cocktail.

Evolution of cocktails

In the time that followed, the more familiar types of the cocktails began to take shape. The early twentieth century would become the golden era of the cocktail and gave rise to *the cocktail hour*, the ritual of cocktail drinking where patrons elected to enjoy cocktails at certain times of the day and in mixed company.

In 1917, Mrs. Julius S. Walsh Jr. of St. Louis, Missouri coined the term "cocktail party". A whole etiquette was built up around the cocktail party. Drinks were served before a meal, and cocktail dresses and lounge suits were worn.

During the golden age of cocktails, glamorous stars Old Hollywood and the Silver Screen were often shown smoking and sipping their cocktails. Later, during American Prohibition (1920-1933), the manufacture and sales of alcohol was outlawed, but it wasn't illegal to drink it; liqueur-based cocktails with fun names like *The Bee's Knees* became popular. Later, during WWII, rum was easily accessible from Latin America, Cuba and the Caribbean (unlike whiskey and vodka, which were affected by rationing)and drinks like the Hurricane and the daiquiri were created. Later, in the 1950's, people enjoyed gin-based cocktails like the martini. This trend continued into the early 1960's when cocktails began to decline in popularity, maybe because the Baby Boomers decided that drinking cocktails was for the older generation.

But popularity would surge again in the early to mid-2000s, which saw the rise of cocktail culture through the artful stylings of mixology, where traditional cocktails were mated with novel ingredients in new techniques. Cocktails became cool again!

Curiosities about cocktails

Here are some crazy cocktail facts and other curiosities.

The largest cocktail ever made was by Nick Nicora in 2012 in Sacramento, California. He set a Guinness World Record with a 10,499 gallon margarita.

The most expensive cocktail in the world was designed by The Ritz-Carlton Tokyo. Their "Diamond Is Forever" Martini features a one-carat diamond alongside Absolut Elyx Vodka. If you order it, this martini will set you back ¥2 million, or roughly $18,500 USD.

The oddest cocktail–and potentially the most biohazardous–ever invented was the Sourtoe Cocktail; it features an amputated, mummified toe and was invented in Dawson City, Yukon Territory, Canada. Originally served during the 1920's, the cocktail was brought back to The Sourdough Saloon's menu in 1973 and has been enjoyed by the bravest of drinkers ever since. (Don't worry. The toes are donated by their owners for the saloon's use.)

The most complicated cocktail for a bartender to make is The Commonwealth cocktail which contains 71 ingredients to honor the 71 countries competing in the 20th Commonwealth games.

Sheldon Wiley once made the most cocktails in the shortest amount of time. He made 18 cocktails in one minute to achieve the World Record in 2013. But believe it or not, he also managed to make 1,905 cocktails in an hour in 2014.

Despite it going strong in other areas of the United States, when alcohol was banned from 1920-1933, Prohibition was never enforced in some places like Kansas City, Missouri.

From the 1960's until 2018, bartenders in Utah had to prepare drinks behind a curtain or partition, out of view of guests. This was called the "Zion Curtain law". It was done to reduce the temptation of excessive drinking.

All Scotch is *whisky*, but it's never *whiskey*. That's because the word is spelled differently in Scotland than it is in other countries.

Believe it or not, absinthe, long been portrayed as a dangerous, hallucinogenic, and addictive substance is a popular cocktail ingredient with its own myths and rituals. Anise-flavored and jade green in color, it's been called "the Green Lady" and– due to its extreme alcohol content–rumored to cause violence, delirium and even death. For that reason, it was made illegal in the early 1900's but the ban was lifted, at least in the US, in 2007. Interestingly, absinthe was also used as a malaria drug before it was banned.

In Canada for almost 100 years it was illegal to alter a spirit for a cocktail, and bartenders weren't allowed to age or infuse spirits purchased for use in Canadian bars. This law only recently changed in 2018.

Chapter Three: The Beauty of Mixology

What is Mixology?

Simply put, *mixology* is the skill of mixing cocktails and other drinks. But mixologists might consider it to be too simplistic a definition. Perfecting the art of mixing ingredients in their perfect balance does take skill, but that seems rather vague. What skills exactly do mixologists require in order to create the perfect cocktail? What I will share with you in this book is exactly what mixology is, how it is different than just mixing and pouring drinks, but how you could be well on your way to developing your own skills as a mixologist.

Mixology itself is an artform. More than just bartending, it requires skillful technique and has a bit of a learning curve. But as mixologists become more skilled in the art of cocktail mixology, new worlds of creativity open up.

This includes the creation of the smoked cocktail. Not only does it provide a new and amazing visual aesthetic, it also brings an interesting taste that many cocktail drinkers say makes any traditional cocktail recipe even better. That's exciting! As you saw in the previous chapter, some cocktail recipes have been around for decades; adding a new element that makes a familiar cocktail fresh and different is what makes this smoked mixology fad so popular.

The first smoked cocktail was invented in the Manhattan bar, *Tailor*, back in 2007. So this fad isn't as new as you might think. Barman Eben Freeman mixed infused smoked cherry and alder wood with their house-made Coca-Cola syrup and bourbon to make an updated Jack and Coke. His clientele was impressed and kept coming back for more. Ever since, every skilled mixologist wanted to learn this skill and every cocktail drinker wanted to try it.

Remember, mixology is an artform to be experimented with and many bartenders have their own take on traditional recipes. A perfect example of this is the classic cocktail, the Old Fashioned. But now, the old is made new as the *Smoked*

Old Fashioned. That cocktail is a natural fit to smoking because of its smoky taste. Whiskey lovers tend to prefer flavors within the savory arena. Interestingly, because of this creativity, recipes may vary in their ingredients from bartender to bartender, and from region to region. A bartender might often have a signature creation, which is similar to a traditional recipe with the same name but it can taste very different because of the artistry in how the drink is prepared.

The cool thing is, this has become the latest at-home hobby. In fact, it's something at-home mixologists on YouTube love perfecting, so it's not just for bartenders anymore! But if you are new to mixology, and in fact have never made a cocktail in your life, this book provides some valuable information to help you get started.

Bartending - what's different?

As I said previously, mixology is more than just bartending. But what exactly is the difference? The truth is any skilled bartender can become a mixologist, but not every mixologist is a bartender. By this, I mean–often, bartending requires lively interaction with clientele, and a knowledge of a good pour, but mixology is a culinary artform not practiced by all bartenders. To be a mixologist, you need more than just a basic knowledge of how to mix and pour a cocktail. While many bartenders know how to make a Vodka Tonic, or any other basic cocktail on the local bar's menu, a mixologist has their own signature cocktails that they've perfected, and has mastered many other difficult to make, lesser known cocktails.

I wouldn't go as far as making the comparison that a bartender and a mixologist are like a waiter versus a chef. But a more culinary approach to drink making is usually in a mixologist's repertoire. That isn't to say that many accomplished bartenders don't have the skill sets to be mixologists. They only need more time and practice (and books like this) to help them create that perfectly-mixed signature cocktail.

The term *mixologist* itself suggests a certain puffiness, like tacking a Ph.D. to the end of your name. In some ways, it's a well-deserved distinction for someone of skill.

But in others, it suggests that the perfect cocktail is a secret formula that mixologists don't want you to know. But I can share that secret with you here and now, and you will find it's not all that earth-shattering.

The secret of a perfect cocktail

When you ask a mixologist the most important thing to remember when creating the perfect cocktail, they'll say one word: *balance*. Balance means the perfect ratio of flavors in every sip, the perfect combination of ingredients. Creating this balance often means a couple of things. First, the drink cannot be too acidic. Second, it shouldn't be too sweet. And third, the cocktail must also not be too bitter. So a great cocktail is a combination of pleasing flavors, one not overpowering another and with the just right amount of alcohol.

This is known as *the golden ratio*. It's the perfect combination of ingredients in the right amount of parts. Often it's two parts liquor, one part sour (usually lemon or lime juice), and one part simple syrup. In most cases, using this formula will guarantee that any cocktail you make will be delicious.

Basic rules for delicious cocktails

Some consider making a cocktail a valuable skill. Others an art form and still others, a science. But whichever way you look at it, the act of making a cocktail can be fun, and easy, if you know the basics. It's in perfecting new types where the challenge comes in. So how do you make a cocktail?

Often you only need a few ingredients, and many cocktails are made the same way.

These are some common steps:

1. First, carefully read the cocktail recipe and ensure you have all the required ingredients.
2. Next, make sure you have a lot of supply of ice, as most cocktails require shaking with ice or pouring over ice.

3. It helps if you use a unique or fancy cocktail serving glass (bonus points if it's chilled).
4. Prepare the garnish. We talked a bit about what these garnishes typically are, and many cocktail recipes require that you prepare them in a particular way. Just follow the recipe directions!
5. Next, use a measuring chart to carefully measure and pour ingredients into your mixing glass or cocktail shaker.
6. Next, add that all-important ice to the mixing glass or cocktail shaker, as the recipe requires.
7. Then mix (or build, or stir, or shake, whatever the recipe calls for) all the ingredients.
8. Then, the-second-to-last step: pour (or strain) the mixed ingredients into the cocktail serving glass (over ice, if it's that kind of cocktail).
9. And last but not least, decorate with the lovely garnish you prepared.

Cocktails and some of the most important spirits you should know for smoked cocktails

This section includes popular alcohols used in cocktails, as well as popular recipes perfected by many mixologists.

Each recipe states the typical ingredients and then how many ingredient parts go into each recipe. Then, the recipe steps include how to create each cocktail specifying when to do what as far as mixing ingredients, straining, shaking with ice and how to serve in a glass, adding garnishes.

The most popular alcohols to include are as follows:

❖ Rum

Rum is produced in the Caribbean as well as North and South American countries. It also comes from sugar-producing regions, like the Philippines and Taiwan. Rum is made by fermenting and then distilling sugarcane molasses or sugarcane juice. The distillate is then aged, usually in oak barrels.

❖ Whiskey & Bourbon

Whiskey is a distilled alcoholic beverage made from fermented grain mash. Depending on the variety, it might be made using either barley, corn, rye, or wheat. It can be aged in wooden casks, sherry casks or casks made of charred white oak.

Scotch whisky is made exclusively in Scotland, primarily from malted barley that is heated over a peat fire and then aged for three to four years in oak casks.

Bourbon derives from America and is a type of barrel-aged whiskey distilled from corn.

❖ Vodka

Vodka is produced in Poland, Russia, Ukraine and even Sweden. You make vodka by distilling liquid from fermented and cooked mashes made from corn, barley, rye, wheat or even potatoes.

❖ Brandy

Brandy is produced by distilling wine and sometimes aged in wooden casks. It generally contains 35–60% alcohol by volume. It originated from France and was originally used medicinally. It is now traditionally consumed as an after-dinner *digestif*.

❖ Vermouth

Vermouth is a fortified wine. It is aromatized and flavored with various botanicals and sometimes shows up in different colors. It was first produced in 18th century Turin, Italy.

❖ Gin

Gin is distilled from juniper berries. It originated in southern France, Flanders and the Netherlands as a medicinal liquor made by monks and alchemists.

❖ Tequila & mezcal

Tequila is distilled from the blue agave plant. It originated around the Mexico city of Tequila 65 km northwest of Guadalajara as well as the Jaliscan Highlands in western Mexico.

Mezcal is distilled from any type of maguey (an agave plant found in the desert). The word *mezcal* means "oven-cooked agave".

❖ Sherry

Originating from the city of Jerez de la Frontera in Andalusia, Spain, Sherry is a white fortified wine. It is often used in cooking, but some prefer the taste of a dry sherry to standard wine.

❖ Cointreau & Triple Sec

Originating in Saint-Barthélemy-d'Anjou, France, cointreau is an orange-flavored liqueur. It is consumed as an apéritif and digestif and is an ingredient in many popular cocktails. Cointreau is sometimes confused with triple sec, but the difference is the type of orange peels used for flavoring and the alcohol content of each. (Cointreau has a content of 40%; triple sec has from 15% to 30%.)

❖ Campari & Aperol

An Italian apéritif, Campari is infused with herbs and fruit in alcohol and water. Its dark- red color categorizes it as bitters.

A type of Campari and with an 11% alcohol content, Aperol is an Italian bitters apéritif made of gentian, rhubarb, and cinchona.

Here are some recipes for commonly made cocktails:

Old Fashioned
(whiskey, spirits, sugar, water, and bitters)

Mix spirits and sugar. Pour syrup, water, and bitters into a whiskey glass. Stir to combine ingredients, then place the ice cubes in your glass. Pour over the ice and add garnish. (Take a look to the recipes n°1, n°8 and n°9: Smoked Old-Fashioned)

Dry Martini
(dry gin, dry vermouth, and orange bitters and is best served
with a lemon twist garnish.)

For a dry martini, pour all ingredients into a mixing glass with ice cubes. Stir well. Strain stirred ingredients into a chilled martini cocktail glass. Squeeze lemon for extra flavor. You can garnish with lemon or olive. You can pour over ice (on the rocks) or serve it straight. Instead of stirring there is the shaken variation. (Take a look to the recipes n°5 and n°51: Classic Brown Derby, Smoked Espresso Martini)

James Bond recipe: "Shaken, not stirred"

Whiskey Sour
(a mixture of whiskey, sugar, and lemon, some recipes call for egg white)

These are the ingredients and their parts: 1 1/2 oz. (3 parts) Bourbon whiskey, 1 dash egg white (optional), 1 oz. (2 parts) fresh lemon juice, 1/2 oz. (1 part) Gomme syrup. To prepare a whisky sour, shake with ice. Strain the shaken ingredients into an ice-filled old-fashioned glass and serve on the rocks. (Take a look to the recipes n°15 and n°39: Whiskey Sour Mocktail, Fresh Peach Bourbon Sour)

Manhattan
(traditionally: parts whiskey, one part sweet vermouth, and bitters.)

Rye is the traditional whiskey of choice, but other commonly used whiskies include Bourbon, Canadian whisky, Tennessee whiskey, and blended whiskey. Here are the parts and preparation: 2 oz. Rye or Canadian whisky, 3/4 oz. sweet red vermouth, dash Angostura bitters, stirred over ice, strained into a chilled glass. Garnish with a maraschino cherry and serve straight-up. (Take a look to the recipes n°2 and n°32: Smoked Manhattan, Smokey Big Apple)

Mojito
(rum, lime, mint, and sugar)

Parts and preparation are as follows: 1 1/2 oz. white rum, 1 oz. fresh lime juice, 2 teaspoons sugar, 6 leaves of mint, soda water. The mint sprigs are mixed or "muddled", more specifically–crushed or pressed in a glass with a wooden cocktail muddler or a wooden spoon–with sugar and lime juice. Add the rum, then top with the soda water. Serve on the rocks. The standard garnish is *yerba buena*–the "good herb", usually a sprig of spearmint.

Margarita
(1 oz. cointreau, 2 oz. tequila, 1 oz. lime juice/mixer)

Rub the rim of the glass with a lime slice, then dip the glass edge in kosher or sea salt. Add ice to your shaker with other ingredients and shake, then carefully pour into the glass without disturbing the salt. Garnish with the lime slice and serve on the rocks. (Take a look to the recipes n°23 and n°41: Smoked Lemon Margarita, Smoked Blueberry Margarita)

Gin and Tonic
(gin, tonic water, various mixers)

The ratio of gin to tonic varies according to the strength of the gin, the taste, and how many other drink mixers are added. But most recipes call for a ratio between 1:1 and 1:3. Ingredients and preparation: 1 part to 3 parts gin (to taste), 3 parts tonic water. Pour in a glass filled with ice cubes. Can use a variety of garnishes, including lime, grapefruit, strawberries, melon or even cucumber. (Take a look to the recipe n°52: Watermelon and Mint Gin & Tonic)

Negroni
(Campari, gin, sweet red vermouth)

Originating in Italy as an aperitivo (carbonated, bitter, and low-alcohol beverage), this cocktail is made of one part gin, one part vermouth rosso and one part Campari.

It is traditionally garnished with orange peel. The negroni is stirred, not shaken, and poured over ice in an old-fashioned or rocks glass. You can even add a slice of orange for some sweetness. (Take a look to the recipe n°43: Blood Negroni Cocktail)

Sazerac
(rye whiskey, cognac, absinthe, sugar cube, bitters)

Parts and preparation are as follows: 1 1/2 oz. Rye whiskey or Cognac, 1/4 oz. Absinthe, one sugar cube, three dashes Peychaud's Bitters. Rinse a chilled Old Fashioned glass with the absinthe, and add crushed ice. Set aside. Stir all of the remaining ingredients over ice. From the prepared glass, remove the ice and discard any excess absinthe from the prepared glass. Strain the prepared drink into the glass. Garnish with a lemon peel.

Bloody Mary
(vodka, tomato juice, worcestershire sauce, hot sauces, garlic, herbs, horseradish, celery, olives, celery salt, black pepper, lemon juice, lime juice and celery salt)

Combine vodka, tomato juice, salt, worcestershire sauce, hot sauces, garlic, herbs, horseradish, black pepper, lemon and lime juice, plus a pinch of celery salt with ice into a shaker and shake gently. Strain into a glass, and garnish with olives and celery (Take a look to the recipes n°47 and n°50: Bourbon Bloody Mary, Smoked Bloody Mary).

Cosmopolitan
(vodka, triple sec, cranberry juice, lime juice)

Parts and preparation are as follows: 1 1/2 oz. vodka citron, 1 oz. cranberry juice, 1/2 oz. Cointreau, 1/2 oz. fresh lime juice. Add all of these ingredients into a cocktail shaker filled with ice. Shake it well and double strain into a large cocktail glass. Garnish with a sliced lime wheel.

Daiquiri
(1/2 oz. white rum, 1 oz. lime juice - any citrus juice, 1/2 oz. simple syrup)

Pour all of these ingredients into a shaker filled with ice cubes, then shake it well. Strain it into a tall, chilled cocktail glass. Serve it straight-up and garnish with half a lime slice. You can also make daiquiris in many other flavors.

Tom Collins
(2 oz. London dry gin, 1 oz. lemon juice, freshly squeezed, 1/2 oz. simple syrup, club soda to top)

Add the gin, lemon juice and simple syrup to a Collins glass. Fill with ice, top with club soda and stir. Garnish with a lemon wheel and maraschino cherry (optional). (Take a look to the recipe n°3: Smoked Tom Collins)

If you are reading this book, you no doubt have tried your hand at home bartending, which is a fun way to entertain your family and friends, but also a great way to have fun and experiment with different kinds of cocktails from the comfort of your own home. Again, it's important we continue to differentiate between mixology and bartending. I discussed a bit about what makes mixology and bartending different on the surface, mostly by defining the difference between what a mixologist does and what a bartender does. But are there more differences?

Essentially, it's the approach you take. If you plan on being a professional mixologist, you would have to do more than take your standard bartending course. But if you simply want to engage in home bartending, you can practice what mixologists do on your own time, with your own experimenting. You can take your time and really evaluate how to improve your mixologist skills, and how you can bump yourself up from bartender to cocktail artist.

If this is your interest, I will share with you some notes on flair bartending and home bartending below.

Home bartending

You can't call yourself a home bartender without a place to tend bar. It serves you best if you have a bar station. A quick on line search can show you simple, less expensive bar carts and stations and more elaborate formal bars–whatever suits your style and needs. But ultimately, all you need is a place where you can store all of the essentials, and mix and serve your drinks.

I mentioned previously the essential spirits needed, but as you know there are many more items that make the home bartending experience fast, easy, and pleasurable. So along with the essential spirits, you will also want to have all of the essential mixers on hand, including tonic water, cranberry juice, tomato juice for a Bloody Mary, some Margarita mix, simple syrup, sour mix, grenadine, and Angostura bitters.

Mixers and spirits are not the only things you'll want on hand. You will want to have and store a few different ways to make ice because if you want to keep on trend, you probably will want to "up your ice game".

You might be wondering what difference does the ice make to a cocktail; I can assure you, it makes an amazing difference! For example, you should use crushed ice for cocktails that need dilution, like daiquiris and other "island" drinks. But if you were to make a spirit-heavy drink like an Old Fashioned or a Manhattan, you would want to use large, round cubes which melt slowly and don't dilute the cocktail which is meant to be slowly sipped. If you load them up with crushed ice, your guest might consider that a bit amateurish.

In fact, a knowledgeable patron (and bartender) would know that certain types of cocktail may even come served with their own signature type of ice. Most notably, the Tom Collins usually comes served with long, rectangular "Collins spears". If you serve a Tom Collins without these, again it might appear you don't know what you are doing. So a great purchase for your home bar station might be a few different molds for the different kinds of cocktail ice.

Another thing for your home bar station is a juicer, so that you can squeeze your own fresh juice to include in your drinks; some kits come with a juicer included. The reason is that fresh juice from lemons, limes, and oranges tend to make more delicious cocktails than store-bought, pre-made juices. Also–added benefit!--once you've squeezed that fresh lemon, you can use the rind to decorate your glass by perfecting something many skilled bartenders and mixologists have in their back pocket: the citrus twist.

For many mixologists and bartenders this is bartending 101, and a pretty basic skill to master, so it's best to learn it as soon as you can. Using either a vegetable peeler or a sharp knife (ideally a paring knife), cut out a thin, oval-shaped slice of peel. Make sure it's free of bruises or blemishes. Remember, a mixologist is an artist; it's all about the visual! You'll want to "hang" the twisted, cut rind on the edge of the glass or, put it on top of the drink and let some of it drape over the side.

As you learn more about how to perfect the making of cocktails, you will want to start filling your toolbox with all of the tools you need, like the paring knife and cutting board for cutting garnishes and fruit. Another necessity for your home bar is a bucket to store ice in, and a shaker and strainer; you will need all three of these to make a standard cocktail. Also, because you now know how important it is to accurately measure your drinks, you may want a jigger to help you measure liquids. A mixing glass and stirrer will come in handy, as not all cocktails are shaken, and you may have some requests for drinks to be stirred instead of shaken, as people have their preferences. For more information about the tools you might want to purchase, refer back to the mixologists toolkit in chapter one.

And speaking of personal preferences, seasoned drinkers will want their cocktails served to them in their correct, signature glass. You'll want to start a collection of the appropriate martini glasses, shot glasses, margarita glasses, highball glasses, rocks glasses and coupes.

Flair bartending

Often when people think of skilled bartending, they may be reminded of a popular fad from a few decades back: flair bartending. And while this seems to have fallen out of fashion in your corner bar, it came back into favor in the mid-2000's in more high-end establishments with skilled bartenders and talented mixologists. This is especially true in tourist spots, where people expect to be entertained.

As a matter of fact, there's even a World Flair Association that has a worldwide league. There are even flair bartender competitions, like The Roadhouse World Finals in London. So if you want to be a professional bartender or mixologist, it's important to remember that flair bartending can still be considered a mainstream discipline that you might need to have within your skill set.

What's important to remember about flair bartending is that it's all about the artistry and the visual. And, while patrons want to see flair bartenders flipping a bottle, they also expect that bartender to create the perfect Old Fashioned, or craft the perfect garnish. The ultimate experience for the bar patron is all about the visual aesthetic, mixed with the perfect taste. That's what good bartending is all about and it's also why smoked cocktails are now so popular.

Chapter Four: Smoked cocktails: The new frontier

In the last chapter, I talked about flair bartending. It might have seemed to only gain popularity due to Tom Cruise in the movie, *Cocktail*; wannabe flair bartenders sought out classes to perfect this skill. But flair bartending is just as popular as ever, and the fad isn't going anywhere. The appeal of flair bartending is that it attracts crowds. It has a visual appeal that makes patrons stop and notice what you are doing, but also order the drinks they want to see you make. This is definitely true of the smoking cocktail "fad"; its popularity is due to the fact that it always garners interest and people want to see it made. So, those who wish to learn how to smoke a cocktail can excite their patrons by learning how to do it for more than one type of cocktail. Having at least 2-3 smoked cocktail recipes on hand in your home bar will excite anyone with discerning tastes. They probably have their go-to cocktail they like drinking, and they have probably seen it made the same way a hundred times. What's great about smoking cocktails is that you can show them a new way of making it and it's a way that has just as much visual appeal as a flair bartender flipping and catching a bottle.

With that in mind, smoking cocktails could very well be the next frontier of mixology and home bartending. But that means more people need to learn about and ask for them. Who better to teach a cocktail connoisseur about them than *you*? If you could perfect a great smoked cocktail, you could turn cocktail drinkers onto something new and exciting. But how do you start? I've talked a bit about spirits, tools, and recipes, but what about the actual smoking? How is it done? Well, read on and find out.

Smoking technique and equipment

I talked a bit earlier about what equipment is typically used when creating a cocktail and what to obtain when you want to make a special smoked cocktail. In this section I will share very specific details about the technique of smoking a cocktail, as well as how exactly to use the equipment you have acquired. In further sections, I will explain the different types of accessories and addons needed to perfect the taste and presentation of the smoked cocktail. I will only share with you what is best recommended to ensure you have the best smoking experience.

First, create your cocktail

First of all, once you fully understand and perfect this technique, repeating it is quite simple. At least, that's what expert mixologists say. As long as you perfect the art of creating the smoke and applying it to the glass, you will have a great effect to use every time you make a cocktail to serve.

Remember, a very important part of making the perfect smoked cocktail is having the perfect cocktail to begin with. Take the steps I have shared with you and attempt to perfect your favorite cocktail. Mix for taste. Keep trying until you have something you are really proud of. Most of the steps required for this are for making the drink, so it's best you learned how to do that first.

Do you have the perfect cocktail made? Great!

Next, how to smoke your cocktail

Stir your cocktail with ice to dilute and cool it. The temperature has to be ice-cold in order for the maximum smokey effect.

Then, create the smoke in your decanter by burning the sticks or chips of your choice in the wood you feel would bring the best flavor to the drink. Experimenting and learning is part of the appeal.

Unplug the decanter, which should now be filled with smoke, and slowly pour the cocktail you made into the smoke. You're going to want to shake this together just a few times, and remember not to shake too hard, too fast, or for too long. Three or four gentle shakes is best if you want to avoid drowning the cocktail in smoky flavor.

Finally, pour the cocktail into the specified serving glass (for that particular cocktail) and wait for the smoke to settle on top.

And that's it! You've smoked your very first smoked cocktail. Remember the perfect smoked cocktail will not just be about the smoky presentation, but it will also have a wonderful aroma and a great taste.

Here are some other ways to smoke your cocktail

- Creating a smoked/torched garnish
- Smoking the cocktail contents themselves
- Smoking the cocktail glass itself, otherwise known as smoke-rinsing the glass
- Using a cocktail smoker, or smoke-rinsing the glass and cocktail together

Here is also a short explanation of each process

Smoking/torching the garnish:

Collect the appropriate complementary garnish such as cinnamon sticks, star anise, dried fruits, cloves, or woody herbs like rosemary, lavender and thyme. Light the garnish on fire. You'll want a small, controlled burn. Extinguish the flame and, while it is still smoking, place the garnish on the rim of your filled cocktail glass to serve. You can even drop the garnish in the drink to infuse the taste. It's that simple. This would be a great technique to try when first starting out.

Smoke-rinsing the cocktail:

This is the technique that requires adding smoke to a container and then bathing your glass in the smoke-filled container. You will have to collect wood chips, or other woody cocktail ingredients, a smoke board, or loose leaf tea to create the smoke to "rinse" your cocktail. Instead of using a smoking box, or glass dome, you can use a large-mouthed Mason Jar.

Using a cocktail smoker:

Cocktail smokers that sit atop a glass and allow you to add smoke to the glass. Essentially with this technique, you add smoke to the cocktail once it has been poured into the serving glass.

This way you get a bit more flavor by adding the smoke to the cocktail directly. This step requires a cocktail smoker of your choice plus the necessary chips (preferably flavored) for burning.

Smoke-rinsing the glass:

Chill the glass and add the garnish if the recipe calls for it. (Smoke "sticks" to chilled glasses best.) Set the combustible materials on a heat safe surface and light them on fire. Once a flame is showing and smoke starts being generated, set the prepared glass on top of the flame to extinguish it. Let the cocktail glass sit and steep with the smoke while you prepare the cocktail. Once prepared, lift your cocktail glass slowly and fill with ice if needed. Pour your cocktail and serve.

Wood to choose

We've discussed different types of wood and wood chips in previous sections. When it comes to woods to use, it turns out every mixologist has their particular preference. Let's get more in-depth about the types of woods mixologists use to complement and perfect specific types of cocktails. The most frequently used woods are: apple wood, hickory, cherrywood, pecan, maple, bourbon-soaked, oak, or mesquite.

Any drink that requires whiskey would be best-smoked with anything that complements its flavor, depending on the type of whiskey used. For example, a rye whiskey goes best with oak, cherry, or hickory to compliment its spices. So a cocktail that requires a rye whiskey ingredient, such as the Manhattan, would be best smoked with these wood choices.

However, you're not limited to burning wood. You can be creative and look for unique blends and tastes to make your own signature cocktails. For example, some mixologists suggest smoking Bourbon with corn husks to really smoke out that corn flavoring. You can try different things to create different and unique flavors, like herbs, certain kinds of fruits and seeds, all-natural tobacco or even your favorite blend of tea! What kind of herbs and wood blend can you try to add even more flavor depth to your favorite cocktail?

Below are some traditional combinations that will get you started in determining what best goes with what.

Syrups to choose

I will share with you a chart of the best syrup, fruit, seed and spirit combinations. But for now, keep in mind these top-shelf syrups to add to your collection:

The 7 Best Cocktail Syrups in 2022

1. Best Overall: BG Reynolds Orgeat.
2. Best Widely Available: Monin Lychee Syrup.
3. Best for Old Fashioneds: Small Hand Syrups Pineapple Gomme.
4. Most Versatile: Giffard Aperitif Syrup.
5. Best Orgeat: Small Hands Food Orgeat Syrup.
6. Best Fruit: Liber & Co Passion Fruit.

Fruits to choose

Here are some great fruit and spirit combinations to keep in mind for when you are building your cocktails. Try experimenting with these combinations:

Spirit	Fruit
Rum	Pineapple
	Coconut
Champagne	Oranges
	Peaches
	Mango
	Watermelon
	Raspberries
Vodka	Strawberries
Brandy	Cherries
	Oranges
Bourbon	Peaches

Adding seeds, nuts, and other items and flavors:

To make your own seed cocktail, use seeds from watermelon, sunflower, muskmelon, chia, flax, pumpkin, sesame or hemp. Blended together they make for a nutty, crunchy taste and can be stored in airtight jar.

Fruit, Herbs, Nuts, and Spirit Combinations

Attempt experimenting with the following chart and see what combinations go best together in relationship to any recipes you find, or simply cater to your tastes.

Fruit	Herbs & Spices	Nuts	Spirits
apple	allspice	almond	Armagnac
apricot	cardamom	hazelnut	Bourbon
blackberry	cinnamon	pistachio	Cognac
cherry	cloves	pecan	Cointreau
cranberry	coriander	pine nut	Kirsh
currant, date	cumin	chestnut	Madeira
lychee	ginger	walnut	Rum
mango	lavender	cashew	Sherry
orange	mint	brazil nut	Vermouth
passion fruit	macadamia	macadamia	Tequila
pear	nutmeg		Brandy
pineapple	rosemary		Champagne
plum	saffron		Vodka
pomegranate	star anise		Gin
pumpkin	thyme		Whiskey
quince			Aperol
raspberry			
strawberry			
watermelon			

Smoked ice

What do you usually need to smoke ice for a smoked cocktail? Not much.

- 1 tray ice cubes
- Wood chips for smoking (in various flavors--choose the one best for your recipe)
- Stovetop or electric smoker (or use a smoking gun)

When you have these three items, you just need to follow these steps: Following instructions of your smoker, heat wood chips until they begin to smoke. Set a dish of ice in the smoker, cover, and smoke until ice has melted; this usually takes from 10 to 20 minutes. Alternatively, you can arrange 1/2 cup wood chips on one side of the pan lined with aluminum foil. Use your handheld kitchen torch to burn your wood chips until smoking.

Why smoke your ice? First, it's the easiest way to create a smoked cocktail. The ice melts providing the smoky taste. If you want the ice to melt faster, use smaller ice. If you want the ice to melt less quickly. use larger ice. All ice smoking can be done either by burning wood chips or using a smoker. This makes the process which requires very few ingredients a breeze.

Tips and suggestions for a perfect cocktail

Is there such a thing as a perfect cocktail? Expert mixologists would say resoundingly *yes*. Here are some tips for creating the perfect cocktail before we move on by providing you even more details for best practices.

1. Create a perfect balance of tastes. I mentioned previously that patrons love cocktails that all have one thing in common: a balance of tastes. That means you should always attempt to use the perfect ratio when mixing. Use a 1:1:3 ratio with alcohol to flavoring when mixing and you should always be bang on with your balance.
2. Always use the best juices. This means no substituting with anything less than 100% juice. Freshly squeezed is best. Also have a variety of fruit juices

on hand, even some you might not see everyday. This is bound to wow your patrons.

3. Go with unsweetened seltzers rather than your typical sodas. This will give your cocktails a more high-end taste. Especially if you are creating a cocktail known for its bubbly taste, opt for something sparkling rather than your average brand name soft drink.

4. Always use whole fruits. Since you make freshly-squeezed juice at your home bar station, you should have a few whole fruits on hand. You could even keep some frozen that may be out of season. These fun fruits cool down your cocktails and give the patron a nice snack to eat once they finish their drink. For those looking to not drink too much, the fiber from the fruits will also help fill them up, so they'll be less likely to drink more than they should.

5. Make your own 'simple syrup.' In order to make simple syrup at the bar mix a 1:1 ratio of water and sugar and boil down until thickened. If you can't make your own, substitute by using your 100% fruit juice and add a little pure stevia.

Smoking cocktails categories

Stirred Cocktails

Stirred cocktails are drinks such as Martinis, Manhattans, and Gimlets. Stirred cocktails can be served straight up, meaning without ice; or on the rocks, meaning with ice. In either case, the drink is mixed with ice and then strained; drinks on the rocks are strained into a glass with fresh ice.

Sours

Sours are mixed drinks containing a base liquor, lemon or lime juice, and a sweetener (simple syrup or orgeat syrup). Sours can be made with just about any spirit: whiskey, vodka, gin, tequila, and brandy.

Highballs

A Highball cocktail consists of two-ingredients such as two to three ounces of base alcohol mixed with usually four to six ounces non-alcoholic mixers. Examples of highballs include scotch and soda, gin and tonic, the Seven and Seven, screwdrivers, Fernet con coca, and rum and coke.

Flips, Fizzes, Swizzles, and Smashes

These are variations of cocktail categories. Some are unique such as the flip, which is any drink that contains an egg. A fizz is just what it sounds like: any drink that has fizzy water added to it (usually served in a tall Tom Collins glass). A swizzle is always stirred with a swizzle stick until the glass becomes chilled. And a smash is a short, julep-like mixed drink, served over ice.

Classic recipes

1. Smoked Old-Fashioned (and smoked ice)
2. Smoked Manhattan
3. Smoked Tom Collins
4. Boulevardier Cocktail
5. Classic Brown Derby
6. Penicillin Cocktail
7. The Poof!
8. Smoked Orange Old Fashioned with a twist
9. Whistlepig Smoked Old Fashioned

Non-alcoholic

10. Hipster
11. Apples to Apple
12. Saratoga Buck
13. Norisan Mocktail
14. Sleight of Hand
15. Whiskey Sour Mocktail
16. Boston Sour Mocktail
17. Gingered Up Zero Proof Sour
18. Kentucky Mule Mocktail
19. Highball Mocktail

Sparkling cocktails

20. Smoked Raspberry Bubbler Cocktail
21. Smoked Cinnamon Apple Sparkling Sangria
22. Smoked Maple Orange Old Fashioned
23. Smoked Lemon Margaritas
24. Harvest Sparkle Drink (Champagne Whiskey Cocktail)
25. Sparkling Punch

Fruity cocktails:

26. Hazy Sunset
27. Smoked Pimm's Cup
28. Holy (Pop) Smokes
29. Alabama Slammer
30. The Whiskey Smash
31. Paper Plane Cocktail
32. Smokey Big Apple
33. Grilled Peach
34. Peach Bourbon
35. Southern Summer Peach
36. Early Autumn Peach
37. The Best Fresh Peach Bourbon Cocktail
38. Smoked Peach Maple Bourbon Smash
39. Fresh Peach Bourbon Sour
40. Smoked Cherry Bounce
41. Smoked Blueberry Margarita

Flavorful cocktails:

42. Fall Rye Whiskey or I'm Not Bitter
43. Blood Negroni

44. Taco Truck Old Fashioned
45. Willie Nelson Smoked Old Fashioned
46. Wake N' Bake
47. Bourbon Bloody Mary or I Love you, Mary Jane
48. Up in Smoke
49. Grilled Orange Smokey Old Fashioned
50. Smoked Bloody Mary
51. Smoked Espresso Martini
52. Watermelon and Mint Gin & Tonic
53. The Deputy's Dilemma
54. Smoke Break

Ideas for the cocktail presentation

Non-alcoholic

For non-alcoholic drinks, the emphasis is on the balance of flavors. A lovely garnish will add a bit of fun. Try citrus twists, citrus wheels/slices, fruit wedges, cocktail cherries, fresh herbs and leaves, salted/sugared glass rims, skewers, and dehydrated fruits.

Classic

Just as some cocktails are classics, so are the garnishes that go with them. Some of the most common cocktail garnishes include maraschino cherries, stuffed olives, citrus wedges, orange slices and whipped cream. Every mixologist or home bartender should have at least these garnishes always on hand for classic cocktails.

Sparkling

For sparkling drinks, keep it classy and simple. Usually one garnish is best. Add a dash of Angostura bitter onto a sugar cube and drop it into a champagne flute. Or you can garnish with an orange slice or a maraschino cherry or even a whole strawberry or raspberry.

Fruity

For fruity cocktails, think fruity garnishes. These include: citrus slices, wedges, and wheels. Cocktail cherries (maraschino, brandied, etc.), pineapple wedges or chunks and melon wedges or balls are always delicious. You can even place something like half a passion fruit, floated on top of the drink.

Flavorful

For flavorful smoky cocktails, it's best to add the item that is creating the flavor. For example, if you want more smoky flavors, add smoked, burnt or charred garnishes or modifiers to your drink. Another option is to burn or smoke herbs and spices like sage, rosemary, or cinnamon sticks, then use them as the garnish to add rich and even more smoky aromas and tastes to the glass

Chapter Five: Smoked cocktails recipes

Classic recipes

1. SMOKED ICE RECIPE AND SMOKED OLD FASHIONED

(This receipt is a twist on the classic Old Fashioned, but using smoked ice.)

- ❖ Prep Time: 15 minutes
- ❖ Cook Time: 2 hours
- ❖ Servings: 1 cocktail

Equipment:

- ★ Mesh strainer,
- ★ Old Fashioned glass

Ingredients:

- Smoked ice*
- 2 quarts water
- 1 large smoked ice cube
- 2 oz. Bourbon
- ½ teaspoon sugar or 1 sugar cube
- 4 dashes Cherry Bitters
- 2 smoked maraschino cherries
- *For the garnish:* 1 orange peel slice about 2 inches long

Building and smoking your cocktail:

First, what you will need to do is strain the water. You do this by using a fine mesh strainer. Then you distribute the water into ice cube molds to freeze into cubes. Using a large rocks glass, combine the sugar, bitters bourbon and mix together. The final step is adding your smoked ice cube. For the garnish you can use your orange peel and top off with your smoked cherries.

---

*<u>Please note how to smoke ice for future recipes</u>:

Preheat your smoker to 200 degrees Fahrenheit. Next, fill a large glass bowl with water. Place on the smoker and smoke for 2-3 hours until the color begins to change from clear to a light yellow. At about the two-hour mark, taste to determine whether you need additional smoke/flavor.

---

2. SMOKED MANHATTAN

The Manhattan cocktail is considered a timeless classic. This whiskey cocktail has a sweet but sturdy flavor, and it holds up to smoke.

- ❖ Prep Time: 5 minutes
- ❖ Servings: 1

Equipment:

- ★ Martini glass
- ★ smoking gun, shaker, strainer, and bar spoon or iced tea spoon

Ingredients:

- 2 oz. rye whiskey
- 1 oz. sweet vermouth
- 2 dashes Angostura bitters

Building and smoking your cocktail:

The first step is to pour all of your ingredients into a mixing glass filled with plenty of ice. Stir with the spoon for 30 seconds. Strain the mixture into a smoke-filled Old Fashioned glass. To smoke the cocktail, use your blowtorch to light the flavored chips and sticks you have chosen. Then you will need to turn your glass upside down to let the smoke fill the inside and stick to the interior of the glass. Wait until the smoke dissipates, then pour your cocktail into the glass.

It is necessary to agitate this mixture for 30 seconds and then let sit for another 3-5 minutes. You can use a cherry as an optional garnish.

3. SMOKED TOM COLLINS

This Smoked Tom Collins is crafted with a smoked basil simple syrup to accentuate the gin's vibrant botanicals while making it smooth as a lemon-lime soda.

- ❖ Prep Time: 5 minutes
- ❖ Servings: 1

Equipment:

- ★ Collins glass
- ★ Shaker, mason jar

Ingredients:

- 2 tbsp smoked basil simple syrup
- 1/4 cup gin
- 2 tbsp lemon juice
- ice
- 1/4 cup club soda
- Smoked ice
- *For the garnish:* lemon slice, basil leaf

Building and smoking your cocktail:

Make a batch of smoked simple syrup and steep in a mason jar with basil leaves. Combine the simple syrup, gin, lemon juice and ice in a cocktail shaker. Shake for 15-20 seconds. Fill a tall, narrow glass with smoked ice. Strain the cocktail into the glass. Top with club soda. Garnish with a lemon slice and basil leaf.

4. BOULEVARDIER COCKTAIL

❖ Prep Time: 5 minutes
❖ Servings: 1

Equipment:

★ Old Fashioned glass
★ paring knife, mixing glass

Ingredients:

- 1 ½ oz. bourbon whiskey
- 1 oz. sweet or semi-sweet red vermouth
- 1 oz. Campari
- Ice, for serving
- Smoked ice
- *For the garnish:* Orange peel

Building and smoking your cocktail:

The first step to this recipe is to combine the bourbon whiskey, sweet vermouth, and Campari. To best combine, use a cocktail mixing glass but any other type of glass will work. Add to the mixture 1 handful of ice and continue stirring for 30 seconds.

Use your paring knife to remove a 1″ wide strip of an orange peel. You can add the oils of the orange peel by squeezing it into the drink. For an extra flourish and tastiness, run the peel around the edge of a lowball glass. Add smoked ice, then strain the drink into the glass. If desired, you can add the oil of the orange peel by squeezing into the drink, or just garnish with the peel and serve.

5. CLASSIC BROWN DERBY COCKTAIL

❖ Prep Time: 5 minutes
❖ Servings: 1 cocktail

Equipment:

★ Chilled Martini glass
★ shaker

Ingredients

- ¾ oz. honey syrup
- 1 ½ oz. freshly squeezed grapefruit juice
- 3 oz. bourbon whiskey
- *For the garnish:* grapefruit slice

Building and smoking your cocktail:

In order to build your cocktail, combine the bourbon, grapefruit juice, and honey syrup into a cocktail shaker. Fill the shaker with ice and shake it until the drink is cold. Finally, strain the shaken mixture into a cocktail glass that you have bathed in smoke. If desired, garnish with a grapefruit slice left over from when you squeezed the juice.

6. PENICILLIN COCKTAIL

❖ Prep Time: 5 minutes
❖ Servings: 1 cocktail

Equipment:

★ Old Fashioned glass
★ muddler or wooden spoon, shaker

Ingredients:

- 2 oz. blended scotch
- ½ oz. single malt scotch
- 4 thin slices of ginger, peeled and about 3/4 inch round
- 1 oz. fresh lemon juice
- ¾ oz. honey syrup
- Smoked ice
- *For the garnish:* candied ginger or ginger root, lemon peel

Building and smoking your cocktail:

In order to build your cocktail, you will need to gently muddle the ginger with a muddler or wooden spoon in the bottom of a cocktail shaker. Do this until the ginger is mashed and juices are released; this should take about 15 seconds. Next you will need to add the blended scotch, lemon juice and honey syrup, along with a handful of clear (non-smoked) ice. Shake this mixture until it is cold. To smoke this drink, you simply need to strain it into a lowball glass with one large clear, smoked ice cube. Create a layer of single malt scotch on the top by carefully pouring it over the back of a spoon just above the surface of the drink. Garnish the glass with candied ginger, ginger root or lemon peel when serving.

7.   THE POOF!

- ❖ Prep Time: 5 minutes
- ❖ Servings: 1 cocktail

Equipment:

- ★ Cognac glass
- ★ Stirrer

Ingredients:

- 1 oz. apple brandy (Copper & King suggested)
- 1 oz. rye whiskey (Bulleit)
- 1 oz. sweet vermouth
- 2 dashes Angostura bitters

Building and smoking your cocktail:

This cocktail is very simple. You just need to stir together all the ingredients. To smoke, you simply need to add to a smoked Cognac glass.

8. SMOKED ORANGE OLD FASHIONED WITH A TWIST

❖ Prep Time: 5 minutes
❖ Servings: 1 cocktail

Equipment:

★ Old Fashioned glass
★ Smoke infuser, stirrer

Ingredients:

- 2 oz. straight rye or bourbon whiskey
- 1 sugar cube
- 2-3 dashes Angostura bitters
- *For the garnish*: cherry, twist of orange peel

Building and smoking your cocktail:

The first step to building your cocktail is to simply place your sugar cube and orange peel in a small bowl, then cover with a layer of plastic wrap. You can immediately start smoking the glass by inserting the tube from the smoke infuser to fill the bowl with smoke. Cover again with plastic wrap, and let it sit for one minute. Repeat if you wish to add extra smokiness. Take the smoked sugar cube and place it in a whiskey glass. You can then soak in the bitters while also adding a little water. Muddle all of these ingredients until the sugar is dissolved. Stir in ice cubes and whiskey. Finish off with a twist of orange peel and cherry.

9. WHISTLEPIG SMOKED OLD FASHIONED

- ❖ Prep Time: 5 minutes
- ❖ Servings: 1 cocktail

Equipment:

- ★ Old Fashioned glass
- ★ Smoking box, stirrer, mixing glass

Ingredients:

- 0.5 oz Runamuk Farms Maple Syrup
- oz WhistlePig Piggy Back 6 Year old Rye
- Balboa Bay Resort
- 0.5 oz Runamuk Farms Maple Syrup

Building and smoking your cocktail:

To build the cocktail, you will first need to put all of your ingredients into a mixing glass. Next you will need to add ice and stir for exactly 25 seconds. Strain and pour over ice. To smoke the cocktail, place the drink in the smoking box and smoke with burning pecan wood.

10.HIPSTER

(Recipe courtesy of Michael Timmons, beverage director at *Merakia* in New York)

- ❖ Prep Time: 5 minutes
- ❖ Servings: 1 cocktail

Equipment:

- ★ Old Fashioned glass
- ★ Shaker

Ingredients:

- 2 orange wedges
- 3 dashes of hibiscus water
- barspoon of apricot jam
- ¾ oz. lemon juice
- ¾ oz. Guajillo chile syrup
- 1.5 oz. Earl Grey tea
- Dash of chili salt
- Smoked ice
- *For the garnish*: orange wedge

Building and smoking your cocktail:

Put all of your ingredients with your smoked ice into a shaker. Shake on the rocks. Then, add an orange wedge for your garnish.

11. APPLES TO APPLE

(Recipe courtesy of Jon Howard, lead bartender at *Henley* in Nashville)

- ❖ Prep Time: 5 minutes
- ❖ Servings: 1 cocktail

Equipment:

- ★ Old Fashioned glass
- ★ Shaker

Ingredients:

- 1.5oz green apple juice
- 1 oz. ginger
- ¾ oz. lemon
- Smoked ice
- **For the garnish:** grated cinnamon or burnt cinnamon stick

Building and smoking your cocktail:

Shake and strain all ingredients. Serve on smoked ice with a dehydrated apple slice garnish, or burnt cinnamon stick.

12. SARATOGA BUCK

(Recipe courtesy of Jason Stevens, beverage director at *Hattie's* in Austin, Texas.)

- ❖ Prep Time: 5 minutes
- ❖ Servings: 1 cocktail

Equipment:

- ★ Old Fashioned glass
- ★ Shaker

Ingredients:

- ¾ oz. guava jam
- ¾ oz. lime juice
- 1oz. ginger beer
- 1.5 oz. seltzer
- Crushed smoked ice
- *For the garnish:* sprig of mint

Building and smoking your cocktail:

Combine all ingredients, except seltzer, and shake. Single strain mixture into a rocks glass. Add seltzer, stir, and top with crushed smoked ice. Garnish with a sprig of mint.

13.NORISAN MOCKTAIL

(Recipe courtesy of *Zuma* Las Vegas.)

❖ Prep Time: 5 minutes
❖ Servings: 1 cocktail

Equipment:

★ Highball glass
★ Shaker, muddler or wooden spoon

Ingredients:

- 8 mint leaves
- 20mL fresh passion fruit pulp with seeds
- 40mL pineapple puree
- 30mL orange juice
- 10mL simple syrup
- smoked ice
- *For the garnish:* passion fruit and mint sprig

Building and smoking your cocktail:

To build your cocktail, you will need to muddle mint your mint with a muddler or wooden spoon. Then you will need to add all other ingredients into a cocktail shaker filled with ice and shake. Strain and pour into a highball glass filled with smoked ice. You can finish off by garnishing with passion fruit and a mint sprig.

14.SLEIGHT OF HAND

(Recipe courtesy of Devon Tarby at *Bibo Ergo Sum* in Los Angeles.)

❖ Prep Time: 2 days (to steep tea and refrigerate tea, sugar and wine tannin powder)
❖ Servings: 1 cocktail

Equipment:

★ Old Fashioned glass
★ smoking gun

Ingredients:

• 5oz. cold brewed August Uncommon "Breathless" Black Tea (or other)
• 0.5 oz. Seedlip Spice
• 1 teaspoon Demerara sugar
• 1 teaspoon wine tannin
• ***For the garnish:*** cherry

(For the Cold Brewed Black Tea: 15 parts black tea leaves, 1 part water: Measure by weight. Let steep for 24 hours. Strain through tea strainer/fine strainer. Keep refrigerated.)

(For the Demerara Sugar: 2 parts Demerara sugar, 1 part water. Measure by weight. Dissolve over low heat. Keep refrigerated.)

(For the Wine Tannin Powder: 25 parts wine tannin powder, 1 part water. Measure by weight. Whisk together until combined. Keep refrigerated.)

Building and smoking your cocktail:

Build the cocktail in an Old Fashioned glass and garnish with smoked cherry wood using your smoking gun.

15. WHISKEY SOUR MOCKTAIL

- ❖ Prep Time: 5 minutes
- ❖ Servings: 1 cocktail

Equipment:

- ★ Old Fashioned glass
- ★ Shaker

Ingredients:

- ¾ oz. lemon juice
- Optional: 1 dash of smoked chili bitters, or another bitter you choose
- 2 oz. non-alcoholic bourbon or whiskey
- ¾ oz. simple syrup
- Smoked ice
- *For the garnish*: lemon peel and/or cocktail cherry

Building and smoking your cocktail:

To build your cocktail, you will first need to add spirit-free whiskey, lemon, bitters (if using), and simple syrup into a cocktail shaker filled with ice. Next, you will need to shake it for about 10-12 seconds. Smoke your ice. Strain the cocktail into an ice-filled, chilled cocktail glass and garnish with a lemon peel and cocktail cherry.

16. BOSTON SOUR MOCKTAIL

❖ Prep Time: 5 minutes
❖ Servings: 1 cocktail

Equipment:

★ Old Fashioned glass
★ Chilled coupe glass, shaker, glass dome, Apple board or Maple board

Ingredients:

• ¾ oz. simple syrup
• ¾ oz. egg white or aquafaba
• 2 oz. non-alcoholic bourbon or whiskey
• ¾ oz. lemon juice
• Optional: 1 dash of smoked chili bitters, or another bitter you fancy
• *For the garnish*: lemon peel and/or cocktail cherry

Building and smoking your cocktail:

In order to build this cocktail, you will need to combine all ingredients listed into a cocktail shaker filled with ice and shake it for 10-12 seconds. If you have one, use a latte whisk for about 10-15 seconds or until the cocktail is creamy, with a head of foam on top. Pour the shaken and whisked mixture into a chilled coupe glass or Old Fashioned glass and use a cocktail cherry and lemon peel to garnish.

The inventor of this cocktail suggests a couple of "fun substitutions" to make this whiskey sour recipe your own. These include substituting maple syrup or honey syrup for the simple syrup. You can also substitute fruit syrup in place of the simple syrup. Great fruit syrup flavors include watermelon, cinnamon, strawberry, peach, ginger or blackberry. Overall, these make amazing flavor combinations to add to a whiskey sour, spirit-free or not! Also, keep in mind that peach, cherry, ginger or smoked chili bitters are other great selections to use for a non-alcoholic cocktail.

Burn atop your desired board under a glass dome. Serve immediately.

17.GINGERED UP ZERO PROOF SOUR

❖ Prep Time: 5 minutes
❖ Servings: 1 cocktail

Equipment:

★ Old Fashioned glass
★ shaker

Ingredients:

- 2 oz. non-alcoholic whiskey
- ¾ oz. lemon juice
- ¾ oz. ginger syrup
- 2 dashes of ginger bitters
- 2 dashes smoked cinnamon bitters
- Cinnamon stick
- *For the garnish*: candied ginger and lemon twist

Building and smoking your cocktail:

To build your cocktail, you start by combining your ingredients into a cocktail shaker filled with ice. Then shake for 10-12 seconds. Light cinnamon stick and let burn. Strain all your liquid into a rocks glass filled with ice and add your garnish.

18.KENTUCKY MULE MOCKTAIL

❖ Prep Time: 5 minutes
❖ Servings: 1 cocktail

Equipment:

★ Copper mug

Ingredients:

- ½ oz. lime juice (or juice from one wedge)

- 2 oz. bourbon or whiskey non-alcoholic alternative
- High-quality ginger beer
- Smoked ice
- *For the garnish:* lime wheel and sprig of mint

Building and smoking your cocktail:

To build your cocktail, first chill a copper mule mug. Next, add your non-alcoholic whiskey. Then, add ½ oz. of lime and continue to fill your mug with smoked ice. You can finish off the cocktail by topping off with ginger beer. Garnish with lime wheel and a sprig of mint.

19. HIGHBALL MOCKTAIL

- ❖ Prep Time: 5 minutes
- ❖ Servings: 1 cocktail

Equipment:

- ★ (Smoke-bathed) Collins glass

Ingredients:

- Juice from one wedge of lemon
- Splash of flavored simple syrup (such as ginger, blackberry, strawberry or fall spice)
- 2 oz. whiskey alternative or non-alcoholic bourbon
- 3-4 oz. of soda or flavored seltzer
- *For the garnish*: fresh herb, berries, fresh citrus (I'm partial to mint, lavender, and lemon verbena as garnish)

Building and smoking your cocktail:

Add non-alcoholic whiskey to a smoke-bathed Tom Collins glass. Next, add your lemon and combine with a splash of simple syrup. Finally, top your cocktail with soda. Garnish with fresh herbs and citrus.

Sparkling recipes

20. SMOKED RASPBERRY BUBBLER COCKTAIL

(This sparkling wine combines both smoky and sweet flavors. A great cocktail for a party!)

- ❖ Prep Time: 5 minutes
- ❖ Cook Time: 45 minutes
- ❖ Servings: 1 cocktail

Equipment:

- ★ Champagne flute
- ★ smoker

Ingredients:

- Pellets: APPLE
- 2 cups fresh raspberries
- Smoked Simple Syrup
- 8 oz. sparkling wine
- *For the garnish:* fresh raspberries

Building and smoking your cocktail:

In order to build this cocktail you will first need to smoke some raspberries. Set your smoker to a temperature of 180°F. Preheat with the lid closed for 15 minutes. Next, you will need to make smoked raspberry syrup. To do so, use a grill mat to smoke 1 cup of fresh raspberries for 30 minutes. After you smoke the raspberries, set a few aside for your garnish. Put the remainder back into a shallow sheet pan and combine with the raspberry simple syrup. Return berries and syrup to the grill grate and let it smoke for an additional 45 minutes. Remove everything from the heat and allow it all to cool. Finally, strain the mixture and refrigerate until ready for use.

To serve: Pour 1 oz. of the smoked raspberry syrup into the bottom of a champagne flute. Top the flute off with sparkling white wine or champagne. Place leftover raspberries onto the rim of the flute to garnish.

21. SMOKED CINNAMON APPLE SPARKLING SANGRIA

❖ Prep Time: 2 hours/1 day (for infusing flavor)
❖ Servings: 6 cocktails

Equipment:

★ stemless wine glass or Old Fashioned glass
★ Pitcher, stirrer

Ingredients:

- 1/3 cup simple syrup
- 1 lemon, sliced
- 1 orange, sliced
- 1 1/2 cups apple juice
- 1/2 red apple, sliced
- 4 star anise
- 1 cinnamon stick
- 1 bottle prosecco, such as Santa Margherita Prosecco Superiore DOCG
- 3/4 cup apple brandy
- *For the garnish*: cinnamon sugar rim, 6 cinnamon sticks

Building and smoking your cocktail:

To build this cocktail you will need to place the apple brandy, simple syrup, lemon slices, orange slices, apple juice, the star anise and the cinnamon stick into a pitcher. Refrigerate and let the ingredients infuse for a few hours, or overnight. Add prosecco and stir.

Before serving, run a lemon along the rim of the glasses and dip into cinnamon and sugar blend. Add plenty of ice to the glass before pouring sangria over. You can place the cinnamon stick in the glass, light it on fire then blow out right before serving as an interesting, exciting, smoky garnish.

22. SMOKED MAPLE ORANGE OLD FASHIONED

❖ Prep Time: 5 minutes
❖ Servings: 1 cocktail

Equipment:

★ chilled Old Fashioned Glass
★ Alder board, kitchen torch, stirrer

Ingredients:

- 1 oz. sparkling apple cider
- 1 teaspoon maple syrup
- 2 oz. of whiskey
- 1 large whiskey ice-cube
- 2 Luxardo Cherries
- a cold splash of water
- orange slice
- 2 dashes of Scrappy's Bitters
- 1 flamed orange disc
- *For the garnish*: cherries or orange peel

Building and smoking your cocktail:

To build and smoke this cocktail, you must first smoke your glass by using a culinary kitchen torch and burning the center of your alder board. Once it's smoking, cover the burnt area of the alder board with your Old Fashioned glass. Once you have smoked the glass, pour in the maple syrup and Scrappy's Bitters. Place in the large whiskey ice-cube. Stir. Add the whiskey and the cold splash of water. Stir. In order to flame your orange peel, tilt it at a 45 degree angle and burn. Rub the burned peel around the rim of the glass before dropping it into the cocktail. Create your garnish by sliding cherries and the orange peel onto your metal garnishing stick and placing in the drink.

23. SMOKED LEMON MARGARITAS

❖ Prep Time: 3-10 minutes
❖ Servings: 1 cocktail

Equipment:

★ Old Fashioned glass
★ Grill or smoker, stirrer

Ingredients:

- 1 oz.
- ¾ oz. lemon juice, smoked or grilled if desired*
- ¼ oz. agave or honey
- 1½ oz. tequila
- sparkling water, to taste*

Building and smoking your cocktail:

In order to build this cocktail, you will need to measure your tequila, triple sec, lemon juice, and agave by adding the parts directly to your glass, and stirring them together. This drink requires plenty of ice cubes, and a top off with sparkling water to taste.

*To smoke or grill your lemons, you will need to cut them in half and put them on your grill or smoker to cook for at least 3 and as many as 10 minutes. You can experiment with how long this will take depending on how smokey you like your margaritas. It might be best to start out with the shorter (3 minute) smoke time and increase each time you attempt to make the cocktail. You can be creative with which sparkling water you use either.

*Good examples of delicious sparkling water are lemon, orange, or raspberry flavors.

24. HARVEST SPARKLE DRINK (Champagne Whiskey Cocktail)

❖ Prep Time: 10 minutes
❖ Servings: 1 or 18 cocktails

Equipment:

★ Pitcher or champagne flute
★ Saucepan, shaker

Ingredients:

- 1/2 cup honey
- 1 oz. whiskey or bourbon
- 1 1/2 cups of the cider honey syrup (entire batch)
- 1/4 teaspoon ground ginger
- 2 1/4 cups prosecco, champagne, or sparkling white wine
- 9 sprigs of rosemary
- 1 tablespoon and 1 teaspoon cider honey syrup
- 1/4 teaspoon ground cinnamon
- 1/8 teaspoon ground cloves
- 1 cup orange juice
- 2 1/4 cups whiskey or bourbon
- 1 extra oz. prosecco, champagne, or sparkling white wine
- Smoked ice
- *For the garnish*: 1/2 sprig of rosemary

Building and smoking your cocktail:

To build this cocktail, you will need to add the syrup you've chosen along with honey, spices, and orange juice to a small saucepan over medium heat. Next, everything must be whisked together until it starts bubbling. Next, remove the mixture from the heat and set it aside to cool for 5 minutes. After 5 minutes, mix the whiskey and syrup together in a pitcher or shaker, along with a good amount of smoked ice, until it is all completely chilled.

Once chilled, strain the mixture into a different pitcher or serving glass. Be careful to ensure that the mixture does not sit in the ice for too long or it'll get watered down. Return the strained whiskey and syrup mixture (no longer on ice) to the refrigerator until you're ready to serve. Just before serving, add the prosecco, garnish with rosemary sprigs, and pour the whiskey/syrup mixture into glasses.

25.SPARKLING PUNCH

❖ Prep Time: 5 minutes
❖ Servings: 1 cocktail

Equipment:

★ wine glass
★ Cherry Wood Chips, smoking gun, punch bowl, wire rack, stirrer

Ingredients:

- ¾ cup fresh lemon juice (about 6 lemons)
- 2 bottles sparkling Shiraz
- 3 liters club soda
- 1 oz. whipping-quality pasteurized egg white, lightly beaten
- 1 ½ cups of St. Germain Elderflower liqueur
- 1 cup of superfine sugar
- 15 mint sprigs
- *For the garnish*: mint sprig

Building and smoking your cocktail:

Brush mint with egg white. Sprinkle with ¼ cup sugar, and let the egged mint dry on a wire rack.

While it's drying, mix your lemon juice with the remaining sugar in a large punch bowl. Keep stirring until all of the sugar dissolves. Insert smoking gun hose to smoke the cocktail. The smoke will need to immerse the drinks for a minute or two. Finally, add your Shiraz, club soda, and liqueur.

To serve, add ice, and your garnish made of sugared mint sprigs.

Fruity recipes

26. HAZY SUNSET

❖ Prep Time: 5 minutes
❖ Servings: 1 cocktail

Equipment:

★ Old Fashioned glass
★ shaker

Ingredients:
- 1-1/2 oz. light rum, such as 10 Cane
- 1/2 oz. overproof rum, such as Lemon Hart Demerara
- 2 oz. pineapple juice
- 1/2 oz. freshly squeezed lime juice from 1 lime
- 1/4 oz. simple syrup
- 2 dashes Angostura bitters
- non-smoked ice cubes for mixing
- Smoked ice cubes
- *For the garnish*: fresh cherry, pineapple chunk, and mint sprig.

Building and smoking your cocktail:

Add both rums, pineapple juice, lime juice, simple syrup, and bitters to a cocktail shaker and fill 2/3 full with non-smoked ice. Shake until well chilled, about 20 seconds. Add smoked ice cubes to a double rocks glass, and strain the cocktail into glass. Garnish with a cherry, pineapple chunk, and mint sprig. Serve immediately.

27.SMOKED PIMM'S CUP

- ❖ Prep Time: 5 minutes
- ❖ Servings: 1 cocktail

Equipment:

- ★ Applewood chips, smoking gun
- ★ cocktail ball

Ingredients:
- 4- 5 cucumber slices
- 6 mint leaves
- 3 oz. of lemon lime soda/ginger ale or ginger beer
- 5 strawberries
- ½ an orange
- 2 oz. of Pimm's No. 1

Building and smoking your cocktail:

In your cocktail ball glass, add mint leaves, oranges, strawberries, and cucumber. Next, add your 2 oz. of Pimm's and 3 oz. of your choice of sodas. The cocktail ball will need to be closed in order to smoke it after the drink is made. Once closed, load the smoking gun and connect the hose to the cocktail ball. Then, turn on the gun and ignite the Applewood chips. Once your glass is full of smoke, turn the cocktail ball and let it all infuse for 30 seconds. To serve, place a straw and add the chopped fruits.

28. HOLY (POP) SMOKES

- ❖ Prep Time: 5 minutes
- ❖ Servings: 1 cocktail

Equipment:

- ★ Old Fashioned glass
- ★ stirrer

Ingredients:

- 1 oz. tequila reposado
- 1 oz. mezcal
- ½ oz. vanilla simple syrup
- ½ oz. Ancho Reyes
- 12 drops Woodford Reserve orange bitters
- 1 tangerine or orange popsicle
- Smoked ice
- *For the garnish*: popsicle, sage leaf

Building and smoking your cocktail:

Combine tequila, mezcal, simple syrup, Ancho Reyes and bitters in a mixing glass and fill with ice. Stir until well-chilled and strain into a rocks glass filled with smoked ice and at least one tangerine-flavored popsicle. The popsicle is tasted and enjoyed as the cocktail is sipped.

29. ALABAMA SLAMMER

- ❖ Prep Time: 5 minutes
- ❖ Servings: 1 cocktail

Equipment:

- ★ Highball glass
- ★ Shaker

Ingredients:

- 1 oz. amaretto
- 1 oz. bourbon (or Southern Comfort)
- 1 oz. sloe gin
- 3 oz. orange juice
- Ice, for serving (use larger ice cubes for smoking)
- Smoked ice
- *For the garnish*: orange wedge and cocktail cherry

Building and smoking your cocktail:

Add the amaretto, bourbon or Southern Comfort along with sloe gin, orange juice, and ice to your shaker and shake until cold. Fill a highball glass with smoked ice, and strain the drink into the glass. If desired, garnish with an orange wedge.

30. THE WHISKEY SMASH

- ❖ Prep Time: 5 minutes
- ❖ Servings: 1 cocktail

Equipment:

- ★ Old Fashioned glass
- ★ Shaker, wooden spoon or muddler

Ingredients

- 1 oz. simple syrup or maple syrup
- Soda water, for serving
- 2 oz. whiskey
- 1/4 lemon, sliced into 2 wedges
- 5 large mint leaves
- Smoked crushed ice, for serving or bathe your glass with smoke

Building and smoking your cocktail:

To build your cocktail, place the mint leaves in a cocktail shaker. Muddle the leaves 4 to 5 times with a wooden spoon or muddler to extract flavor. Next, add your lemon wedges and muddle everything again. Finally, add the whiskey and simple syrup. Fill the shaker with ice and shake until cold. Strain into Old Fashioned glass over crushed ice and add a splash of soda water.

31.PAPER PLANE COCKTAIL

- ❖ Prep Time: 5 minutes
- ❖ Servings: 1 cocktail

Equipment:

- ★ Cocktail glass
- ★ shaker

Ingredients

- 1 oz. bourbon whiskey
- 1 oz. Aperol
- 1 oz. Italian amaro
- 1 oz. fresh lemon juice
- Smoked ice
- *For the garnish:* Lemon peel

Building and smoking your cocktail:

Add the bourbon, Aperol, amaro, and lemon juice to a cocktail shaker. Fill it with smoked ice and shake it until cold. Strain into a cocktail glass. If desired, garnish with a lemon peel.

32. SMOKEY BIG APPLE

❖ Prep Time: 5 minutes
❖ Servings: 1 cocktail

Equipment:

★ Cocktail glass
★ Burnt smoking stick, stirrer

Ingredients:

• Balboa Bay Resort
• 2 oz. Hudson Manhattan Rye
• 0.5 oz. Apple Cider Syrup
• 1 dash Old Forester Smoked Cinnamon Bitters

Building and smoking your cocktail:

To build your cocktail, combine Hudson, Apple Cider Syrup and your bitters into a mixing glass. Next, add ice and stir it all together for 25 seconds. Strain the mixture over one large ice cube. To smoke your cocktail, light a whole cinnamon stick until it starts smoking. Place the stick on top of the ice and serve.

33. GRILLED PEACH COCKTAIL

❖ Prep Time: 20 minutes for cocktail (one month for freezing honey)
❖ Servings: 1 cocktail

Equipment:

★ Old Fashioned glass full of crushed ice
★ Grill, saucepan, grill pan, shaker

Ingredients:

To make your batch of honey simple syrup:
- 1/4 cup honey (inventor suggests local, raw)
- 1/4 cup water

To make your cocktail :
- 1/2 oz. fresh lemon juice
- 1/4 oz. fresh orange juice
- 1/2 oz. honey simple syrup (see instructions)
- 1 fresh, ripe peach, grilled
- Smoked ice
- 1 1/2 oz. bourbon
- *For the garnish:* fresh thyme

Building and smoking your cocktail:

To build this cocktail, you must first create the honey simple syrup. To do so, combine honey and water into a small saucepan and put it over medium heat until it comes to a light simmer. Continue stirring until the honey dissolves into the water. Next, remove the saucepan from the heat and set aside to cool before transferring to an airtight container. Can be refrigerated for up to one month.

For this recipe, you will also need to grill peaches. First, slice your peaches in half; remove the pits. Then, bring a grill pan to medium-high heat. Brush the peaches lightly with olive oil and place flesh-side down into the pan. You will need to ensure the peaches are soft, so flip peaches onto their backs, and grill for another minute or two until the skin and flesh are soft. Each side will need to be grilled until you see grill marks, or for three minutes, whichever comes first.

For building and smoking the drinks, put the grilled peaches into a shaker, muddling them until they nearly disintegrate. Add in all other ingredients, plus a handful of smoked ice. Cover with lid and shake vigorously for at least 10 seconds, attempting to break the ice into chunks.

Finish the cocktail by straining the mixture through the cocktail shaker lid, then through a fine mesh sieve into an Old Fashioned glass that has been filled with crushed ice. Use fresh thyme for a green, aromatic garnish.

34. PEACH BOURBON COCKTAIL

❖ Prep Time: 5 minutes
❖ Servings: 1 cocktail

Equipment:

★ Cocktail glass

Ingredients:

- 1 oz. peach schnapps
- 2 oz. bourbon
- 1 ½ oz. freshly squeezed orange juice (Note: use one orange. Or you can use no sugar-added store bought juice)
- Ice, for serving (try large ice cubes for smoking that melt slowly)
- Smoked ice
- *For the garnish*: fresh peach slice, fresh mint sprig

Building and smoking your cocktail:

Pour the peach schnapps, bourbon and orange juice into a glass. Add smoked ice and serve.

35.SOUTHERN SUMMER PEACH COCKTAIL

❖ Prep Time: 5 minutes
❖ Servings: 1 cocktail

Equipment:

★ Cocktail glass
★ blender

Ingredients:

- 4 oz. lemonade
- 1 whole peach, sliced, with skin removed
- 1 tbsp peach syrup
- 1/2 lime, juiced
- 1 1/2 cup whiskey
- 1 splash mint flavoring
- 1 cup Ice
- Smoked ice
- *For the garnish*: sliced peaches, sliced limes, 1 mint sprig

Building and smoking your cocktail:

Combine smoked ice, lemonade, whiskey, lime juice, peach and peach syrup (use crushed ice this time). Next, add mint flavoring and pulse in a blender Finally, pour your drink into a glass. Garnish with mint springs, or lemon or peach slices.

36. EARLY AUTUMN PEACH COCKTAIL

❖ Prep Time: 5 minutes
❖ Servings: 1 cocktail

Equipment:

★ Cocktail glass
★ Maple and/or apple wood

Ingredients:

- 2 oz. Irish whiskey
- 1 oz. peach lemonade, preferably Sparkling Ice Peach Lemonade
- 1/2 tablespoon maple syrup
- *For the garnish:* peach slice

Building and smoking your cocktail:

Smoke with some maple and/or apple wood to give that fall taste. Pour the whisky and peach lemonade into a glass filled with ice. Add the maple syrup and stir gently to combine. Garnish with a slice of peach. Serve immediately.

37. THE BEST FRESH PEACH BOURBON COCKTAIL

❖ Prep Time: 7 minutes
❖ Servings: 1 cocktail

Equipment:

★ Old Fashioned glass
★ Grill, shaker, stirrer

Ingredients:

- 1 peach

- 1 tsp 100% pure Canadian maple syrup
- 2 oz. Smoked Maple Bourbon Whisky (Knob Creek)
- 3 dashes Angostura Bitters
- 1 sprig of fresh thyme
- 2 oz. non-alcoholic spicy ginger beer (The Great Jamaican)
- 1/2 oz. fresh lemon juice
- 1 oz soda water
- Grilled peach slices
- *For the garnish*: edible flowers, sprig of fresh thyme

Building and smoking your cocktail:

In order to make this cocktail you will have to grill peaches. When you grill peaches, you make the peach even more delicious, but you also soften the peach so that you're able to break it down in the cocktail shaker.

Begin by firing up your grill on high heat. Whe the grill is ready, wash and halve your peach and remove the pit. Coat the peach with a thin layer of maple syrup. Oil your grill (inventor suggests Canola oil). Add peach halve. Cook for 5 minutes, or until a light char appears. If you cannot use a grill, use a broiler instead. If you're broiling, do so for 2 minutes or until maple syrup starts to bubble and caramelize.

Add your grilled peaches into a cocktail shaker along with 8 ice cubes sprig of fresh thyme, bitters, and Bourbon Whisky and shake vigorously until the peaches are broken down. Add four ice cubes to a cocktail glass and strain the contents of the shaker overtop. Top off with ginger beer, lemon juice and soda water. Continue stirring to combine all ingredients. To garnish add your sprig of thyme and/or your edible flowers.

38. SMOKED PEACH MAPLE BOURBON SMASH

A summer-meets-autumn sip juxtaposing juicy late summer fruit with a smoky grilled edge and spicy autumnal warmth.

- ❖ Prep Time: 5 minutes
- ❖ Servings: 1 cocktail

Equipment:

- ★ Cocktail glass
- ★ Grill, shaker

Ingredients:

- 3 dashes Angostura Bitters
- 1 sprig of fresh thyme
- 2 oz. non-alcoholic spicy ginger beer (I used The Great Jamaican)
- 1/2 oz. fresh lemon juice
- 1 peach
- 1 tsp 100% pure Canadian maple syrup
- 2 oz. Smoked Maple Bourbon Whisky (Recipe inventor suggests Knob Creek)
- 1 oz. soda water
- *For the garnish*: sprig of fresh thyme, grilled peach segment

Building and smoking your cocktail:

Grill your peach halves until lightly charred. Then remove from heat and set them aside to cool while you prepare the ingredients in your cocktail shaker.

To do this, add eight ice cubes to the shaker along with your grilled peach halves, bitters, bourbon, and a sprig of fresh thyme. Shake vigorously, until the cocktail shaker becomes cold and the peach is thoroughly broken down. Next, add between five to six ice cubes to your cocktail glass and strain the shaker contents over. Keep shaking to ensure the peach comes through and until your cocktail glass is more than half full. Finish the drink by topping with dry ginger beer, fresh lemon juice and soda water. Garnish with your leftover grilled peach segment, and sprig of fresh thyme.

39. FRESH PEACH BOURBON SOUR

❖ Prep Time: 5 minutes
❖ Servings: 1 cocktail

Equipment:

★ Old-fashioned glass filled with smoked ice
★ shaker

Ingredients:

- 2 oz. bourbon
- 3/4 oz. fresh peach simple syrup
- 3/4 oz. fresh lemon juice
- 2-3 dashes bitters
- 1 cup ice
- Smoked ice
- *For the garnish*: slice peach – fresh or from the sugared peaches, slice lemon, maraschino or amarena cherry

Building and smoking your cocktail:

For the peach bourbon sour. Add the bourbon, peach simple syrup, lemon juice and bitters to a cocktail shaker. Add ice and shake vigorously until the outside of the cocktail shaker is very cold and the drink is frothy, about 30 seconds. Strain into an Old Fashioned glass filled with smoked ice. Garnish with a fresh peach wedge, slice of lemon and/or a maraschino cherry if desired.

40.SMOKED CHERRY BOUNCE

- ❖ Prep Time: 3 hours and 20 minutes (3 months for storing cherry mixture and brandy)
- ❖ Servings: 1 cocktail

Equipment:

- ★ Old Fashioned glass
- ★ Cherry wood chunks, glass smoking dome, stirrer

Ingredients for cherry mixture:

- 6 cups fresh bing cherries (about 1 3/4 pounds), stemmed and pitted, divided
- 2 cups granulated sugar
- 2 tablespoons fresh lemon juice
- 1 quart (32 oz.) brandy or rye whiskey

Building and smoking your cherry mixture

Prepare smoker with cherry wood chunks according to manufacturer's instructions, bringing internal temperature to about 225°F; maintain temperature 15 to 20 minutes. Place 1 cup (about 4 1/2 ounces) cherries in an even layer in an 8-inch square disposable aluminum pan, and place on smoker grates. Close the lid. Smoke cherries by maintaining temperature inside smoker around 225°F, until cherries are infused with desired degree of smoky flavor, shaking pan occasionally, for 30 minutes to 1 hour and 30 minutes. Combine smoked cherries, sugar, lemon juice, and remaining 5 cups fresh cherries in a large saucepan. Bring to a simmer over medium. Reduce heat to medium-low, and simmer, stirring occasionally, until sugar is dissolved and mixture is very juicy, about 20 minutes. Remove from heat, and let cool for 1 hour. Pour cherry mixture into a large, clean lidded jar, and top with brandy. Screw the lid on tightly, and store in a cool, dark place for 3 months.

Ingredients for the cocktail:

- 1.50 oz. bourbon
- 0.5 oz. honey brandy
- 0.5 oz. vermouth blanco
- 1 bar spoon or Tbsp Campari
- 0.25 oz. freshly-squeezed lemon juice
- 0.5 oz. sage simple syrup
- 4 dashes cherry bitters

Building and smoking your cocktail:

Add all ingredients into a mixing glass with ice. Stir until chilled. Place a large ice cube into a rocks glass. Strain liquids into the glass. Place glass in a container for smoking. Smoke the cocktail with the cherrywood.

41.SMOKED BLUEBERRY MARGARITA

- ❖ Prep time: 5 minutes
- ❖ Cook time: 10 minutes
- ❖ Servings: 1 cocktail

Equipment:

- ★ Old Fashioned glass
- ★ Grill, shaker

Ingredients:

- 1 oz. Cointreau
- 2 oz. mezcal
- 1 oz. fresh lime juice
- 7 smoked blueberries
- **For the garnish:** a speared, roasted blueberry and a rosemary sprig.

Building and smoking your cocktail:

To begin making your cocktail, you will need to place washed berries on a cookie sheet in the grill and smoke for 15 minutes. Next, add your blueberries and Cointreau to a shaker to gently muddle, then add in ice and all other ingredients to the shaker and shake. Ensure that you fine-strain the drink over ice into a rocks glass.

Flavorful recipes

42. FALL RYE WHISKEY COCKTAIL (or: I'M NOT BITTER)

- ❖ Prep Time: 5 minutes
- ❖ Servings: 1 cocktail

Equipment:

- ★ Old Fashioned glass with one large ice cube
- ★ handheld blowtorch, Apple wood, stirrer, mixing glass

Ingredients:

- 1.5 oz. Wilderness Trail Rye whiskey
- 1/2 oz. chai spice-infused simple syrup from reduced Regatta Craft Mixers Ginger Beer
- 1 oz. Montenegro Amaro
- *For the garnish*: dried orange slice, cinnamon stick, star anise

Building and smoking your cocktail:

To build your cocktail, combine your ingredients into a mixing glass while adding ice. Stir the ingredients with the ice until everything is chilled and well-combined. Then, you will need to strain the mixture into a rocks glass on top of one large ice cube.

Use your torch to burn applewood and turn the glass upside down to let the smoke bathe the glass. Then pour your drink into the glass. You can garnish the drink with a cinnamon stick, an orange slice, and star anise.

43. BLOOD NEGRONI COCKTAIL

❖ Prep Time: 5 minutes
❖ Servings: 1 cocktail

Equipment:

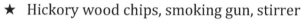

★ Old Fashioned glass with large ice cubes
★ Hickory wood chips, smoking gun, stirrer

Ingredients:

- 1 orange peel (garnish)
- 1 oz. of Gin
- 1 oz. of Sweet vermouth
- 1 oz. of Campari
- *For the garnish:* orange peel

Building and smoking your cocktail:

Add 1 oz. of Gin, Sweet vermouth and Campari into a mixing glass with ice, and stir until chilled.

Once these ingredients are combined, you can pour into a rocks glass filled with large ice cubes. Once prepared, place a drink disk on top of the glass. Load your smoking gun with hickory wood chips and then connect the hose drink disk. After this, turn on the gun and ignite your wood chips until they burn. Do this until your glass is full of smoke. Then, turn off the gun and let it infuse for 30 seconds. You can garnish with your orange peel when you are ready to serve.

44. TACO TRUCK OLD FASHIONED

❖ Prep Time: 5 minutes
❖ Servings: 1 cocktail

Equipment:

★ Old Fashioned glass filled with one large smoked ice cube
★ stirrer

Ingredients:

- 1/4 oz. raw agave nectar
- 2 dashes orange bitters
- 2 oz. tequila reposado if you have it
- ½ oz. mezcal (This will add a lot of smokiness to your drink, so be prepared for the taste. You can substitute with the same amount of tequila to dilute the smokiness.)
- 8 drops Bittermen's Xocolotl Mole bitters
- 1 large smoked ice cube
- *For the garnish:* Add smoked salt or spicy salt to rim the glass. Or use an orange peel.

Building and smoking your cocktail:

To build your cocktail, use an Old Fashioned glass and rim it with spices and salt. For the best results, wet the outside of the rim with an orange wedge, then dip into a bowl of mixed salt and spices. Use a mixing glass to combine tequila, mezcal (if using), agave nectar and bitters. Finally, add your ice and stir until everything is well-chilled.

Strain the mixture into a prepared glass filled with one large smoked ice cube. Garnish with orange peel.

45. WILLIE NELSON SMOKED OLD FASHIONED

❖ Prep Time: 5 minutes
❖ Servings: 1 cocktail

Equipment:

★ Old Fashioned glass
★ Cherrywood, stirrer

Ingredients:

● 2 oz. Woodford Reserve
● 1 Sugar Cube
● 5 Dashes Spicy Cherry Bitters
● 5 Dashes Blood Orange Bitters
● 5 Dashes Black Walnut Bitters
● *For the garnish:* burnt orange peel

Building and smoking your cocktail:

Begin by muddling your sugar cube with your bitters. Once this is done, fill your glass with ice. Top it with Woodford Reserve. To smoke the cocktail, place the glass in your smoker while it burns cherrywood and infuse to taste. Garnish with burnt orange peel.

46. WAKE N' BAKE

❖ Prep Time: 5 minutes
❖ Servings: 1 cocktail

Equipment:

★ Collins glass

Ingredients:

● 1.5 oz. Bulleit Rye

- 6 Dashes Black Walnut Bitters
- Drizzle Maple Syrup
- Cold Brew Coffee
- **For the garnish:** cinnamon sticks

Building and smoking your cocktail:

Light cinnamon sticks on fire and place the lit end under glass. Let the glass fill with smoke, then add ice and all ingredients. Shake, then return to the glass and top with a smoking cinnamon stick.

47.BOURBON BLOODY MARY (or: I LOVE YOU, MARY JANE)

- ❖ Prep Time: 5 minutes
- ❖ Servings: 1 cocktail

Equipment:

- ★ Cocktail glass
- ★ Hickory wood, shaker

Ingredients:

- Top with Smoked Tomato Juice
- *Mix equal parts Worchester Sauce, apple cider vinegar, olive juice, and lime juice.
- 2 oz. Maker's Mark Cask Strength
- 1/2 oz. Bloody Flavoring
- Rim with Smoked Paprika and Sea Salt
- 5 Dashes Celery Bitters

Building and smoking your cocktail:

Rim martini glass with smoked paprika and sea salt; set aside. Smoke the cocktail, by using hickory wood to smoke your tomato juice. Once smoked, fill the shaker with all of your ingredients and strain into the glass.

48. UP IN SMOKE

❖ Prep Time: 5 minutes
❖ Servings: 1 cocktail

Equipment:

★ Smoke-bathed brandy snifter
★ shaker

Ingredients:

- 1 oz. Woodford Reserve Double Oaked
- 1 oz. Copper and Kings Butchertown Brandy
- 1 oz. Cherry Heering
- Top water/orange juice
- *For the garnish*: rosemary

Building and smoking your cocktail:

For this cocktail, you will start with smoking before you build the drink, by lighting one sprig of rosemary and placing it under a glass and letting the glass fill with smoke. Mix the Woodford Reserve, brandy, and Cherry Heering into a shaker, then shake with ice. Strain the drink into the smoked glass filled with ice. For extra flavor, top with orange juice and garnish with rosemary.

49. GRILLED ORANGE SMOKEY OLD FASHIONED

❖ Prep Time: 15 minutes
❖ Servings: 1 cocktail

Equipment:

★ Old fashioned glass
★ Grill, stirrer

Ingredients:

- ½ tbsp Smoked Honey
- 1.5 oz. of bourbon
- ½ oz. of sugar syrup
- Smoked Ice
- Couple of dashes of Orange Bitters
- **For the garnish:** 1 slice of grilled orange

Grilling the orange:

Slice some oranges into ¼" thick round slices. Then char over charcoal for a minute on each side. If the orange gets too floppy, you've either left it too long or sliced it too thin. Make sure it has structural integrity. Once it's ready, you can leave the slices to cool to use in your cocktail.

Building and smoking your cocktail:

Start with a classic whiskey glass. Begin by pouring the bourbon over smoked ice, then adding sugar syrup. Combine the bourbon and syrup over ice. Stir thoroughly to mix, adding in a couple of drops of orange bitters. (The inventor of this recipe suggests Angostura bitters which are also used in the original Old Fashioned recipe.) Add smoked honey and mix thoroughly. You can then add your caramelized orange slice as garnish either to the rim of the glass or you can add the entire slice to the drink itself. The best thing about this drink is as the smoked ice melts, it will change in complexity and smoke flavor.

50. SMOKED BLOODY MARY

The recipe inventor's method uses a smoking gun, but also suggests using a backyard smoker.

- ❖ Prep Time: 5 minutes
- ❖ Servings: 1 cocktail

Equipment:

- ★ Highball glass
- ★ A smoking gun (recipe inventor suggests Breville), wood sawdust, cocktail shaker (if using the smoking gun)

Ingredients:

- 1.5 oz. of vodka
- Tabasco or other similar hot sauce
- Rasher of smoked bacon
- Smoked salt
- Cracked black pepper
- Worcestershire sauce
- Tomato juice
- *For the garnish*: celery stick, rasher of bacon

Building and smoking your cocktail:

Add ice to a highball glass. Pour in the vodka and tomato juice, then add a couple of dashes of Worcestershire sauce, combined with a couple of dashes of Tabasco. Add smoked salt, and ground, cracked black pepper. To garnish, use a crispy rasher of smoked bacon and a celery stick.

51. SMOKED ESPRESSO MARTINI

A staple in clubs and bars, this is a sophisticated, punchy cocktail. But this is also another cocktail you can enjoy in your backyard once you've added a bit of smokiness to it.

- ❖ Prep Time: 5 minutes
- ❖ Servings: 1 cocktail

Equipment:

- ★ Cocktail glass
- ★ cocktail shaker, smoking gun

Ingredients:

- 1 oz. vodka
- 1 oz. coffee liqueur (Kahlua)
- 1 standard shot of espresso
- Ice

Building and smoking your Cocktail

To build your cocktail, start by filling your cocktail shaker about half-full with ice. Next, add other, liquid ingredients. Use your smoking gun to fill the shaker with smoke. Inventor has not found another method of smoking the cocktail, other than to use liquid smoke. Make sure you use the liquid smoke sparingly, with only a drop or two. After you add the smoke, replace the shaker lid and shake vigorously for thirty seconds. Finally, strain everything into a martini glass. (Inventor suggests you enjoy this cocktail with chocolate!)

52. WATERMELON AND MINT GIN & TONIC
(smoked gin & tonic)

❖ Prep Time: 15 minutes
❖ Servings: 1 cocktail

Equipment:

★ Old Fashioned glass
★ Grill, stirrer

Ingredients:

- 1.5 oz. Gin (i.e. Hendricks)
- Tonic Water (i.e. Fever-Tree Mediterranean Tonic)
- Ice
- Watermelon
- *For the garnish*: sprigs of mint

Grilling your watermelon:

To grill watermelon, cut it into ¾" slices, then put it over a raging charcoal grill for 3 minutes. Grill until you see grill marks and a bit of caramelization. Flip and grill the watermelon on the other side, for the same amount of time. Once grilled, cut your watermelon into ¾" cubes. Do this quickly, and close to serving time to avoid mushiness, or store in the fridge after grilling.

Making Your Gin and Tonic

Add ice to a short, heavy-bottomed glass. Add one cube of grilled watermelon to the glass and slightly crush it with the back of a spoon to release some flavor. Add a second piece of grilled watermelon; do *not* crush. Add gin, and top up with your tonic water. Stir lightly to combine flavors. Garnish with a sprig of mint.

53. THE DEPUTY'S DILEMMA

❖ Prep Time: 5 minutes
❖ Servings: 1 cocktail

Equipment:

★ Highball glass
★ kitchen blowtorch, rolling pin

Ingredients

- 1 cup alcoholic ginger beer (not ginger ale)
- A couple of sprigs of mint
- 1 oz. of dark Caribbean rum
- ½ oz. of elderflower syrup
- 1 tsp of brown sugar
- Wedge of lime
- Smoked ice
- *For the garnish*: 1 sprig of rosemary

Building the cocktail

To start building this cocktail, put a couple of mint leaves and a tsp. of brown sugar, and a lime wedge into a highball glass. Muddle together in the bottom of the glass, this time using a rolling pin. Next, put a large cube of smoked ice in the glass. Pour over the rum and elderflower syrup, and top up with the ginger beer. For the garnish, you can use the rosemary sprig. This recipe calls for lighting the top leaves with a blowtorch or lighter until they smolder. For the best effect, serve while it is still smoking, which adds to the delightful aroma and flavor of this drink.

54. SMOKE BREAK

❖ Prep Time: 5 minutes
❖ Servings: 1 cocktail

Equipment:

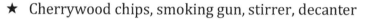

★ Old Fashioned glass with one large ice cube
★ Cherrywood chips, smoking gun, stirrer, decanter

Ingredients:

- 2 dashes Woodford Reserve spiced cherry bourbon-barrel-aged bitters
- 1 dash Angostura bitters
- 2 oz. W.L. Weller Special Reserve bourbon
- 3/4 oz. cream sherry
- 1/2 oz. vermouth
- *For the garnish*: dark chocolate, dried black cherries

Building and smoking your cocktail:

To build and smoke this cocktail you will need to use a smoking gun to light the cherrywood chips. Next, add smoke to a glass decanter, then cover the top. Add in your bourbon, cream sherry, vermouth, bitters and all of the ice into a large mixing glass. Stir until well-chilled. To finish making the cocktail, strain the contents into the prepared decanter. Cap the decanter, watching the drink mingle with the smoke. Pour the finished and smoked cocktail into a rocks glass filled with one large ice cube. For a delicious and fun addition, serve to your guest with a tray of dark chocolate and dried black cherries.

Chapter Six: NOTES

Chapter Seven: Conclusion

Now that you have a long list of recipes to try, remember you can always refer back to this book when you want to find a new recipe, recall what items to use, or remind yourself of any steps you've forgotten when smoking cocktails. You could even use this chapter for a reference. We've also included several blank pages for you to add your own notes.

In the beginning of this book, I asked you to consider who this book might be written for. The overarching idea is that this book is for everyone. Even skilled and talented mixologists who are aware of the smoked cocktail "fad" can still use this book to learn a new recipe or a new tip on how best to smoke a particular cocktail. But the novice home bartender can use this book to learn the same skills. Part of the fun of smoking cocktails is knowing it can be easily done at your home bar station. You can create new and interesting takes on old classic cocktails that your friends and family will love, while also turning them on a new interesting way to order a cocktail. Maybe they will travel to a trendy spot and see one on the menu and ask to try it. Maybe they will even want to learn this new skill.

Even a seasoned bartender who has never branched out beyond serving drinks could purchase a smoking kit for the bar and add a new exciting item to the bar menu. In the end, the reader of this book has all of the knowledge they need to try smoking cocktails today.

There are many ways to smoke a cocktail. The key to creating the perfect smoked cocktail is to remember three things: the balance of taste, new creative approaches to old classics (whether it be a new garnish, or a new flavoring, or simply adding the smoke), and the skill of smoking.

But as you now know, the smoke in a smoking cocktail is just one part of the overall experience. The first and most important step is perfecting the cocktail. This means perfecting taste as well as presentation. You learned the best presentation comes from using the right tools and ingredients, those that are both innovative and expected by the patron. These expectations, from seasoned cocktail drinkers, usually revolve around things such as the color and taste of the cocktail, the ice and garnishes used, and how the cocktail is prepared (whether shaken or stirred, for example). You've learned that you'll need tools for smoking cocktails, and to keep these things on hand: wood chips/shavings, whole spices, nuts, teas, tobacco, and woody herbs like rosemary and lavender. All of these items will often come in handy when you want to create a smoky taste and pleasurable smells, as well as have items to help generate fire and smoke.

Reading this book, you learned detailed and also varied instructions on how to smoke a cocktail. As you've learned, there are a few different ways to smoke a cocktail:

Many mixologists may have only been aware of one way to smoke, and now they have 3-4 different ways, depending on what tools they have at their disposal. I shared with you the various kinds of kits you can buy, but a quick on line search will show you not only what is available to you, but show you the reviews from others who have used the product; they can tell you which method and product they think is best. But ultimately, trying it out yourself is the best way to know the method you prefer. Whether you use a glass dome, a smoking box, or a smoking gun, through experimentation, you're more than likely to find the method you find easiest and most consistent.

When smoking a cocktail you will find it is best to use certain complementary recipes for the best effect. Refer back to the list of recipes in this book, but also to previous chapters (chapter 4 for example) to be reminded of special ingredients sure to enhance the presentation and taste of every cocktail you perfect. From the woods to use, the right mixers and syrups, a go-to combination of fruits, seeds, and other accompanying ingredients, as well as the perfect smoked ice to perfect the blend, you will find everything you need to create the perfect cocktail in the lists I shared with you.

I hope, from this book, you take away the fact that you are capable of creating beautiful and enticing smoked cocktails from scratch. I shared with you early on the definition of a mixologist. And while the concept might seem intimidating to someone who considers themselves a novice bartender, the one thing mixologists have in common is the knowledge of how to make a great cocktail through practice. After reading this book, it would seem you are halfway there already!

There really are only a few slight differences between a bartender and a mixologist. But a great bartender can be a great mixologist, and vice versa. There are three things that will help a bartender become a mixologist: in-depth knowledge of how to mix new, creative cocktail recipes, how to utilize mixologist's tools, and the perfect location and time to practice. It might also help to share your concoctions with someone else to get a second opinion. Keep practicing your bartending skills, perfect your garnishes, know what ingredients go best with what spirits, and you will soon be the envy of your cocktail-loving friends. Even better, now you have this handy trick called smoking to bring the perfect flourish to every new recipe you create.

Image Credit: Shutterstock.com

Made in the USA
Monee, IL
26 November 2023

47422151R00059